Break The Curve

■ SMART STRATEGIES SERIES ■

Break The Curve

The Entrepreneur's Blueprint For Small Business Success

Tim Burns

INTERNATIONAL THOMSON BUSINESS PRESS
I(T)P® An International Thomson Publishing Company

London ● Bonn ● Johannesburg ● Madrid ● Melbourne ● Mexico City ● New York ● Paris
Singapore ● Tokyo ● Toronto ● Albany, NY ● Belmont, CA ● Cincinnati, OH ● Detroit, MI

First Edition 1999
Typeset by Laserscript, Mitcham, Surrey
Printed in the UK by TJ International, Padstow, Cornwall

ISBN 1–86152–319–X
International Thomson Business Press
Berkshire House
168–173 High Holborn
London WC1V 7AA
UK

http://www.itbp.com

Dedication

This book is dedicated to the three women in my life:

My mother, Marilyn S. Downs
My grandmother, Camille S. Scariano
And my fiancée, Denise S. Starr.

And to the memory of Ewing Marion Kauffman, in recognition for both his entrepreneurial talents and his generous contribution to the worthy cause of entrepreneurial education.

Contents

List of figures

List of tables

Preface

The title for *Break the Curve* is based upon the traditional Bell curve, a statistical illustration of test scores and other performance measures for a group. Generally, when individual scores are plotted on a graph, most usually converge to a fairly defined range known as the average, with other scores being scattered both below and above the average. A line drawn through the plotted scores often takes the shape of a bell, since it starts with the lowest score, rises uniformly as the scores approach the average and then drops uniformly to the highest score. This highest score is often referred to as 'setting the curve.' Setting the curve is the goal of many ambitious students. However, in today's competitive marketplace it's not good enough to just set the curve. Instead you want to 'Break the Curve' and attain even higher levels of performance, productivity – and most of all – profits.

This book is written for anyone with the dream of striking out on their own, being their own boss, and creating their own destiny. I truly feel that this is the Age of the Entrepreneur and that the opportunities for self employment have never been better.

The purpose of this book is to provide you with the essential tools of the entrepreneur. This includes a fundamental understanding of the marketing, accounting, legal and financial aspect of your business and how these managerial tools converge in the creation of your business plan. I will also discuss alternative entry strategies to business ownership, such as franchising and buying a business. Also presented will be various self-management techniques, which are the peak performance and high achievement strategies found in the self-development literature, but which seldom appear in business books. However, without adequate self-management skills such as time management, goal setting and emotional resilience, you will have a more difficult time managing the business and confronting its inevitable obstacles.

Entrepreneurship can be a great equalizer. It is available to anyone without reference to age, education, gender or nationality. All it takes is a carefully prepared business plan and a lot of hard work.

In today's rapidly changing economy, the skills of the entrepreneur are particularly valuable. It is these skills that recognize opportunity and make things happen. It is the goal of the book to provide you with the business skills and techniques of the entrepreneur. Once equipped with these skills, you will be in an outstanding position as we head into the 21st century.

Acknowledgments

Let me first acknowledge the patience, support and understanding of my lovely, and sometimes lonely, fiancée Denise, who put up with me during the writing of yet another book. Denise, your smile keeps me going.

I want to also express my appreciation to Julian Thomas, So-Shan Au and Fiona Freel of the International Thomson Business Press for their help and support on this book. I also appreciated the editing assistance of Anne Simpson.

In addition, I am very appreciative of the following people for allowing me to use their material in this books. Let me thank Brian Tracy, CPAE for allowing me to use material from his fine audio programme 'Psychology of Success' in the book. Thanks to Pamela Wegmann for allowing me to use her competitive matrix profile. Thanks also to Melissa Elliott for giving me great insight into the banking industry and to Jody Horner for reviewing the marketing chapters. And thanks to the Professional Association of Innkeepers International for allowing me to use part of their industry study. I also appreciate the help of Gerry Deloume, my secretary at the law firm of Staines, Eppling & Myers, and the support of my other associates. Thanks also to Sarah Davies, a paralegal at Staines & Eppling, for her outstanding proofing. For the artwork, I am indebted to Iguana Graphics and Communications and Claire Wicker, who also does my PowerPoint presentations. Thanks to R. Mack Davis of the Entrepreneurial Education Foundation, who helped me in the proposal, but could also be thanked for his 'suggestions to the manuscript'. Thanks to Alice Kennedy of the Small Business Development Center at the University of New Orleans for her friendship and support. But most of all, many thanks to all of my small business students and clients, who taught me so much about the world of entrepreneurs. The book is for them and the rest of you entrepreneurs out there.

PART I

The basics of entrepreneurship

CHAPTER ONE

Introduction – everyone is an entrepreneur

> The empires of the future are the empires of the mind.
>
> (Winston Churchill)

The entrepreneurship trend is here to stay

Although you may have never thought of yourself as an entrepreneur, today's turbulent economic climate requires that everyone think and act like an entrepreneur. This applies throughout the business world, ranging from the existing business owner to the young person starting their career to the displaced employee and to those currently employed (possibly for now) in organizations. Despite an expanding world economy, the employment world continues to be turned upside down as corporate layoffs persist in dominating financial headlines. As we move into the 21st century and our economy evolves from the Manufacturing Age into the Information Age, the requirement for entrepreneurial thinking and expertise will only increase.

Many experts, such as Peter Drucker, note that the end of the traditional job is at hand. In his recent book, *Managing In A Time of Great Change*, Drucker predicts that the traditional job will be replaced by work teams, which will be subcontracted out from project to project.

These observations point out that the trend toward self employment is not a temporary phenomenon, like the painful downsizings of the early 1980s, but a fundamental shift in the nature of work. Not only are organizations facing the prospect of fewer employees, but those who remain are being asked to perform a greater variety of tasks. The days of the technical specialist are coming rapidly to an end, as large organizations continue to urge their employees to behave more like entrepreneurs.

Entrepreneurship is booming – so don't despair

The solution to this possibly unsettling trend is not to wring your hands and hope that it will somehow all go away. While some industries and jobs are naturally more secure than others, there is no real security in today's economy. Companies that tried to maintain their no layoff policy in this new economy, such as International Business Machines, quickly found themselves in financial trouble. And even those employed by one of the most benevolent companies could have problems if their employer is acquired by one of the least benevolent.

A better approach is to become more entrepreneurial. Simply put, this involves taking a hard look at your experience, resources, education, and interests, and then assessing those skills against today's marketplace in search of a fit. The sooner that you can learn to think in those terms, the sooner you can liberate yourself from the inherent risk in depending on *one* organization for your livelihood and well being. This approach is true even for those who are beginning their career. While organizations can provide excellent experience, remember that you need to manage your *own* career as if it were your *own* business.

Although the security of a large organization can be reassuring, it does exact a price, which is lack of autonomy. Employees essentially put their entire career in the hands of their employer in exchange for job security. Sometimes this works out well for employees, but employees can also find undesirable supervisors, positions and transfers foisted upon them.

This is not to say that corporations are inherently bad or that they are facing imminent extinction. I had some of my best memories and work experience with a Fortune 500 company in the United States. There was a time when I was so energized and excited by what I did, that I scarcely thought about anything else. However, there were the predictable disadvantages to corporate life which included a sometimes negative corporate culture and an unwelcome job transfer.

Self employment is no panacea of pleasure either. I remember the endless marketing, the silent phone, and the many months before I had any significant *gross* revenues. However, in the long run, self employment can provide the best of both worlds, the opportunity to do what you enjoy and the financial security from doing it well. In addition, the entrepreneur also knows that their job security is within their control, instead of some corporate bounty hunter.

Today is an excellent time to be in business for yourself. Advances in technology have evened the playing field in many occupations and industries. Today's consumers are more particular and willing to pay for personal service. This facilitates the creation of niche markets. Many economists predict that as those born after World War II reach their peak spending years, there will be a tremendous boom in the economy, particularly for those in the 'right' consumer niches. In fact, some experts are even proclaiming this era and beyond as the Age of the Entrepreneur and foresee outstanding opportunities ahead for the self employed.

But for many, including myself, the thought of self employment was absolutely horrifying.

But it need not be. Contrary to popular belief, entrepreneurs are not reckless risk takers who eagerly gamble their fortunes away. Successful entrepreneurs take only educated risks. Once you learn and master the tools presented in this book, you will develop skills that will enable you to carefully plan your business and take only educated risks.

Anyone can be an entrepreneur

I firmly believe that virtually anyone who applies the principles set forth in this book can be a successful entrepreneur. Although I concede that some people are more temperamentally suited for entrepreneurship than others, that does not necessarily rule the others out. I dislike the various questionnaires that appear in many business books purporting to assess someone's likelihood of entrepreneurial success. Such 'tests' could unnecessarily discourage those, who, with some attitude adjustment and training, could very well become outstanding entrepreneurs.

For many, that first huge step towards entrepreneurship might require only a change in *belief*. In fact, changing one's belief is the biggest hurdle for the first time entrepreneur, who might have spent much of their career working for others in some comfortable corporate cocoon. To suddenly be on their own is a strange and frightening prospect. This is certainly a normal reaction for anyone who trades in a steady paycheck for something much less certain. However, the fear is lessened for those who are simply willing to *believe* that they can master self-employment skills and succeed as entrepreneurs. Belief in yourself is also important for those who are just starting their careers.

Sceptics are always quick to point out that there is no guarantee of self employment success. And this pessimism is seemingly borne out by business statistics, which relate that three out of four new businesses fail within the first five years. However, these sobering statistics also point out that nearly *all* business failure can be attributed to the lack of knowledge in key business areas, such as finance, accounting, management and law. With proper education and planning, the success ratio can actually be turned in favour of the entrepreneur. Anyone who learns the entrepreneurship tools presented in this book and applies them on a consistent basis can be successful as an entrepreneur.

FIGURE 1.1   Reasons why most businesses fail

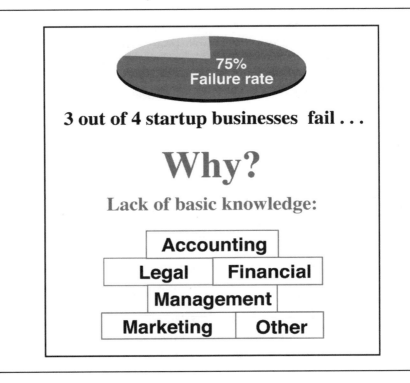

Clearly, there are the natural entrepreneurs, the child prodigies who scorned formal education to pursue some driving passion that consumed them from a young age. Bill Gates, the Chairman of Microsoft is clearly the most famous (and most wealthy) of these. His vision and intense interest in the infant microcomputer industry caused him to drop everything else, including college, to pioneer the operating language for IBM's first personal computer. The rest, as they say, is history.

On the other side of the entrepreneurship spectrum are those whose personality and work ethic would make the self-employment road quite rocky. These individuals are more comfortable either unemployed or underemployed in a soft job and would never even consider the rigours of business ownership. I am not necessarily condemning this conduct, but pointing out that these individuals would probably not make good entrepreneurs.

The large majority of us, including myself, fall somewhere in between. This is the group to which the book is addressed. Some might have great ideas and insights for a new business, but are petrified to start one. Others have no hesitation about plunging boldly into new ventures, but neglect to plan properly. All of us have good tendencies and bad tendencies as entrepreneurs. My point is that anyone with the desire, who is willing to learn, take educated risks and work hard, can start and succeed in their own business. I know this because I had to learn and change my beliefs to become a successful entrepreneur myself.

Entrepreneurship education is critical for the business owner. Although the stereotyped entrepreneur is often portrayed as someone who prefers their own wits to education, this is not necessarily the case. *Break the Curve* offers carefully distilled business and legal concepts which are critical to business success. This distilled knowledge is based on my 15 years of experience practising business, tax and securities law and advising large and small businesses in legal and financial matters. I have also gained useful business insights by teaching and lecturing in the fields of business law, accounting and entrepreneurship. The information is presented in an integrated, logical and systematic format and is designed to help you plan most effectively for business results.

Four elements of the entrepreneur

Being a successful entrepreneur is actually very simple. Not easy, but simple. It requires four major elements:

1   belief;

2   focused knowledge;

3   a proactive approach;

4   perseverance.

With all four elements, one can't help but succeed. But without any one of the four, you're going to have a difficult time.

Simply put, *belief* requires the unqualified belief in your ultimate ability to succeed as an entrepreneur. As elementary as it sounds, this lack of belief is a major problem for many, including myself. Belief is basically

FIGURE 1.2 Four elements of the entrepreneur

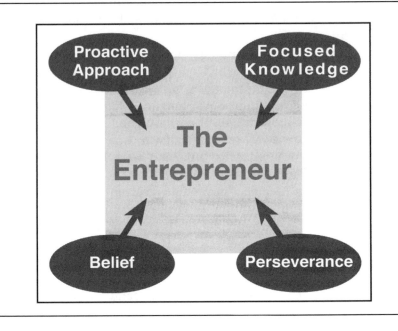

the confidence in your ability and resources. This confidence can be derived from inner faith, past success, or the realization that many others have succeeded before, some with only a fraction of your resources. There are numerous stories of business successes who conquered enormous odds, ranging from immigrants to a country who could not even speak the language to those who had to overcome severe handicaps.

The second requirement for business success is focused knowledge, which this book aims to provide. While any knowledge is beneficial, don't get detoured on the information superhighway. Prioritize your learning within the confines of your particular business or industry or related applications. Knowledge is best utilized if synthesized into a workable plan. Piles of books and periodicals will do little good in your closet. You must be able to quickly access the knowledge and apply the information to your business. Consequently, the preparation of a business plan, which blends together all of your knowledge and insight of your business, is a major focus of this book. In addition, technology is coming to the rescue of those knowledge junkies like myself who fill up bookcases, closets and attics with information. As discussed later in the book, there are several methods of computer information storage which have recently become affordable.

However, all of the focused knowledge and business planning in the world won't accomplish anything if one just sits on it. Instead, you have to be proactive. New ideas or insights have to be quickly implemented or they tend to die on the vine. Learn to make that phone call or send out that letter TODAY, not tomorrow. One also has to be reactive and to make adjustments according to the market. If something isn't working as planned, try another tactic.

But being proactive doesn't mean being *impulsive*. Rather it means taking and synthesizing the information, weighing the alternatives and ultimately acting. Entrepreneurs often make dozens of decisions in a single day. Therefore, they must be comfortable with their decision-making process. Effective decision-making techniques will be discussed later under self management, because all of the business savvy in the world won't help the entrepreneur with poor self-management techniques.

The final requirement for business success is perseverance. There will be bad times. But one must persevere and work through the rough periods. Keeping your faith can be very trying when your livelihood or life savings is at stake. Perseverance requires that you keep a long-term perspective while concentrating in the short term. It is not driving blindly into walls, but rather involves considerable introspection and reflection. Perseverance also requires a good sense of humour and, of course, some backbone. Most importantly, it involves never giving up. Perseverance strategies are also discussed in the self-management section of this book.

My story

I can best illustrate how these principles helped one of the least entrepreneurially inclined people I know by telling my own story. I was indoctrinated in the 'bigger is better' mentality and believed that the good students worked for the large firms and corporations and bad students, well . . . shifted for themselves. Upon graduation I went to work for a medium-sized law firm, but was later recruited to a Fortune 500 Company in the United States. As I was preparing to leave the law firm, a senior partner questioned my decision to work for one company. He cautioned that clients were the only *real* source of a lawyer's job security and that I had exhibited client development potential. He advised that having one's own clients was much preferable to being at the mercy of one company because you never know what might happen. Unfortunately for me, his assessment of the situation proved quite accurate. At the time I was too enchanted by the glamour of the corporate big time to heed the advice.

For a while, the legal big time, with its continual flow of corporate deals, was fantastic. I was literally flying all over the world lawyering complex business transactions which dwarfed anything that my friends were doing. During this time, the company went through several rounds of layoffs, but I was too busy to notice.

Then came the transfer. It just so happened that the legal department needed to shrink by one lawyer at a time when another department head was interested in my heading up governmental affairs at the state capital. The solution was obvious to a new General Counsel, who didn't want to fire anyone. As a result, I was soon banished from the buzzing corporate headquarters to a desolate outpost in a strange city. My travel was truncated from international financial capitals to destinations which were quite local. Initially, I was so dissatisfied by the assignment that I wasn't grateful for the fact that I had survived yet another significant purging by the company.

Then came the earthquake. A major domestic business was sold, a layer of management was put to pasture and one third of the corporate staff was let go. Although I survived, I realized that the company's new focus made my tenure there just a matter of time. But I handled this bad news quite stoically.

Well, not exactly. Actually, I became quite distressed by the prospect of losing my job and frantically scrambled to find another one before the Grim Reaper paid a visit to *me*. Unfortunately, my company's downsizing had been well publicized and many employers treated me like an unwanted refugee. Friends and acquaintances gave me that strange, rueful look usually reserved for condemned prisoners or terminal patients. I avoided the office headquarters, which seemed in a perpetual state of gloom and filled with whispers about pending executions.

One day a very promising legal position for a major local corporation was advertised in the newspaper. The ad didn't mention the company's name, but instructed applicants to mail their résumés to the Human Resources department at a particular post office box. I was *very* interested. With a little ingenuity, I was able to coax the company's identity from an unsuspecting postal employee. That information allowed me to bypass the résumé slush pile by sending mine directly to the company's General Counsel. I phoned the General Counsel soon afterwards, and somewhat bewildered by the apparent coincidence of my letter, he agreed to a quick interview. In preparation, I pored over the company's annual reports, governmental filings and a confidential recent research report on the company smuggled to me by a friend in the securities industry. Afterwards,

I dashed over to the company's office and spent two hours charming and convincing the General Counsel of my ability. The interview went very well. In fact, we were actually in the middle of salary negotiations, when the company's new CEO decided to downsize, despite the fact that the company was already lean and performing well financially. Naturally, the unfilled positions were the easy cuts. I later learned that the General Counsel himself took early retirement.

That episode made it particularly obvious to me that I was going totally against the grain. In pursuing this latest position, I had done everything that the job-seeking books had recommended and perhaps some things not recommended. I finally realized that it wasn't necessarily me, rather the jobs just weren't there. I could continue to bang my head against the wall or adjust to the new reality, which was self employment.

My first hurdle was to believe in myself. Those who spend too much time in comfortable corporate cocoons believe that their entire career and well being is tied to a particular company or one similar to it. They become addicted to the perks and security and find themselves shackled by corporate handcuffs (which range from golden handcuffs for senior executives on down). Sometimes the women hit the glass ceiling and the men become corporate eunuchs. Had I really become a corporate eunuch?

As I struggled to regain my confidence, I thought about someone I had known some time ago. With his shaggy hair and worn jeans, he wasn't that much to look at. He struck me as a little brash and wasn't that smart either because he planned on attending an expensive private university when neither he nor his parents had much money. In fact, he had boldly announced his intentions to everyone. This all seemed particularly ludicrous, since he would have to be in school for many years. But the strange thing about it all was that he succeeded. It wasn't easy and there were many setbacks along the way. But he persisted and somehow managed to finish. It had taken three jobs, a lot of work, student loans and today's equivalent of $150,000 in scholarship assistance. The truth is that he succeeded because he never once doubted that he would.

So I thought . . . if I did it then, I can do it now. I quickly sprang into action and began to plan. I approached law practice as a business and came to appreciate how much technology had radically changed the field.

I joined the Law Practice Management section of the Bar and began reading extensively in the fields of entrepreneurship and business development. I prepared a business plan in which I niched my practice areas and outlined marketing and financial strategies. I raised my profile in the community by hosting a legal show on the local cable television channel and wrote a column on entrepreneurship for a leading business publication.

Eventually I made the formal break as an employee and have never looked back.

The entrepreneur's blueprint

In the pages that follow, I'm going to present the methodology for preparing the entrepreneur's blueprint for small-business success, which is the preparation of the all-important business plan. Each chapter will discuss a portion of the business plan and present a set of Action Steps to prepare the plan. To obtain the full benefit of this book, it is very important that you prepare your business plan. You might want to read through the book once, before actually preparing the plan. However, I urge you to at least take notes at the end of each chapter while some of the ideas are fresh in your mind. You might want to jot down a rough draft of that particular section of your plan. Don't be overly concerned with perfection at the beginning of the preparation of your plan. Focus on getting the ideas down. Some of the items will be very simple to you, while others will require more effort. The important thing is that you make a diligent effort in preparing your business plan – since that truly is *your* blueprint.

The best thing about learning these business planning techniques of the entrepreneur is that they never leave you. Once you master the skills, you can intelligently approach any business situation, including acquiring a franchise or buying a business. Once you learn the fundamentals of business planning, you can even move and establish a business. Entrepreneurial knowledge can be used to plan a second, third, fourth or fifth career. The business management techniques outlined in this book have worked for me as well as my clients. Follow me through this book and I will provide you with the skills and knowledge necessary for you to 'break the curve' and achieve your dreams.

Summary

1   Today's rapidly changing economy requires that everyone be an entrepreneur.

2   Entrepreneurship is booming.

3   Anyone willing to make the effort can be successful as an entrepreneur.

4   The four elements of the entrepreneur are belief, focused knowledge, a proactive approach and perseverance.

CHAPTER TWO

Following your passion: choosing your business concept

> People rarely succeed at anything
> unless they have fun doing it.
>
> (Anon.)

The entrepreneur's ultimate freedom

The best aspect of self employment is the ability to exercise the ultimate freedom of the entrepreneur, which is to choose the particular business that *you* wish to pursue. It is *this* freedom of choice that makes the often trying experience of self employment worthwhile. Despite all the inevitable setbacks and frustrations, you continue to persist, because you are doing what you really enjoy, something in which you find meaning and purpose.

Choosing your business is one of the most important decisions that you will ever make. Therefore, choose something that gives you fulfilment and purpose. There is too much collective unhappiness in the world because people simply don't like their work. Discontent in the workplace invariably spills over into personal lives and affects families.

That is why it is important that you choose a career which you are excited about and it forms part of your vision of yourself as well as your business. I firmly believe that everyone was put on this earth to fulfil a unique purpose in their lives and that they have been given gifts and insights to achieve this purpose. The key is to find a career that allows you to achieve your potential and contribute your unique gifts and talents. As a result, choosing the wrong occupation is not only a waste of your time, but also a waste of your *life*.

If you've already chosen a business that provides you with fulfilment – FANTASTIC! Congratulations are in order because you've already cleared a very important hurdle. But you might want to at least skim this chapter anyway to be sure that your business truly meets the criteria discussed. Remember that choosing your business is the entrepreneur's ultimate freedom and not something to be taken lightly.

However, this great benefit of the entrepreneur, the so-called ultimate freedom, can really present a dilemma for those who are uncertain about self employment in the first place. In some cases, the ultimate freedom can then be transformed into the ultimate curse as prospective entrepreneurs rack their brain for something that they can make a living at. After all, the business world is competitive and certainly no place to indulge yourself in fantasy when there are bills to pay and mortgage payments to meet.

Or is it? For a moment, forget about all that. Forget about your bills, your mortgage, all those sobering statistics about small business failure and ask yourself this one question:

> If I could do any occupation or business in this world, what would it be?

Surely you're not serious. Anything? Yes, anything. What would be your dream job. Close your eyes and think about it for a moment. If you could do anything, what would it be? Often this very critical question becomes lost in the clamour of well-meaning advice from family and friends and our own raging voices of self doubt. Many times we are steered to a business thought of as 'safe.' Still others try to discourage us from going into business for ourselves in the first place.

Choosing a business is not always easy, particularly when it is chosen during an emotional time. Someone laid off in mid career might feel pressured to quickly reenter the workforce and find themselves jumping at the first business opportunity. Financial urgency might push others to try to make something happen quickly. But it is important to resist those urges and engage in some careful soul searching before you plunge in.

The truth is that in today's rapidly changing, downsizing, outsourcing global economy there is no such thing as an absolutely 'safe' business. Things are changing so fast that today's sure bet could become tomorrow's dinosaur. The beginning of the Information Age is having a profound effect on the entire economy. For the first time, industries as secure as university teaching and civil service are experiencing layoffs. The global economy and accelerated advances in technology have produced a rapidly changing economic system. Even companies such as International Business Machines were threatened with extinction and had to change from their no-layoff policy. What happened to the vinyl record manufacturers when compact discs took over the record industry?

Since there's tremendous uncertainty in every business, you'd just as soon choose something that you really enjoy.

Although I try to be optimistic, I am not a blind believer that a positive attitude will get you everything. While optimism is an essential hallmark of the entrepreneur, it does need to be tempered and shaped by the realities of the marketplace. Later, we will discuss marketing as well as finance and accounting. But for now, have fun and ask yourself – if I could have any business or occupation in the world, what would it be?

What would be my dream job?

Learn to listen to your subconscious

The process for choosing your business begins in your subconscious. It is an intuitive decision, something that you feel from the inside. For some, this decision is obvious. They had a passion for a particular area their entire life. Do you think Bill Gates had a passion for computers? Did this passion lead him to become one of Harvard's most celebrated alumni as a dropout? Think of anyone who achieved anything of note, from Madonna to Mozart, from Einstein to Edison who did not have a deep passion about what they were doing.

For many others, choosing their life's purpose is far from easy. They have to set aside years of self doubt to find what they really want. Intuitive decisions, such as career decisions, are best made in a relaxed, reflective environment. Sometimes a career choice has to evolve and involves some risk taking. But the businesses that have endured in this world and that have made a difference were founded with an overriding purpose or VISION. Establishing the vision for your business involves setting your personal vision, which starts with an occupation that you are really interested in. Table 2.1 illustrates some of the myths vs. realities involved in choosing a business.

Love the product or the process

A general rule of thumb in choosing a business is to love either the product or the process. Although this might seem a little idealistic, the cold reality is that it is very difficult to succeed at something that you don't enjoy. Although work will always be work, it is much better to look forward to your workday than to dread it. Your chances of success are much better.

TABLE 2.1 Choosing your business: myths vs. realities

Myth	Reality
1 There are some safe businesses.	1 While some businesses might appear 'safer' than others, the subtleties and dynamics of a competitive marketplace make it difficult for any business to be considered completely safe.
2 Some businesses (particularly in the technology area) require specialized training or advanced knowledge.	2 Of course, you don't just set up an Internet service provider overnight, but the learning curve in the technology area is becoming increasingly shorter. You can also subcontract out the more technical tasks.
3 Three out of four new businesses fail in the first five years.	3 While many of these reports on business are sobering, the great majority of business failure (90%) can be attributed to lack of fundamental business skills, such as accounting, marketing and management. Businesses that take the Premier FastTrac® programme report an excellent success rate.
4 Someone trying to start a business doesn't have the luxury to indulge themselves in the business of their choice.	4 The entrepreneur who wants to succeed in the long run, needs to do something they enjoy. Starting your own business is difficult enough without the added burden of not liking what you do.
5 Consult outsiders and experts for their opinion on which business to start.	5 Expert advice has a short shelf life. Your mission is to become as knowledgeable as possible about your potential business. Solicit input, but make your own decision.
6 Select only businesses in the 'hot' growth areas.	6 While growth trends are certainly very important, be careful about jumping blindly into the current 'hot' industry. It is better to select your type of business and then tailor it to growth and economic trends.
7 Figure out all of the subtleties of business before deciding on one.	7 Decide on the type of business that you are interested in generally and then refine it with a business plan.

FIGURE 2.1 Choosing your business: love the product or the process

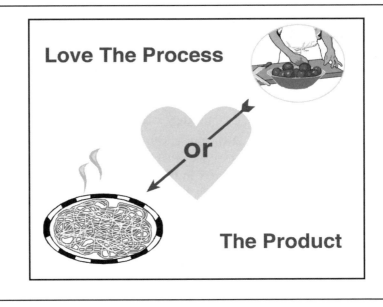

A successful business can be built around your interest in a particular product. These products could be something as diverse as jewellery, clothes, heavy equipment, computers and, of course, food. This product could be an outgrowth of a hobby or interest that you've always enjoyed. Many interests or hobbies, particularly at an early age, provide important clues about desired career paths. In addition, the constantly evolving computer industry is supplying a multitude of possibilities for creative and technical products. Think of the burgeoning web industry that just a few years ago was not even in existence.

Alternatively, you can also build a career out of a particular process. For example, you might enjoy face-to-face selling to people. You might then find any career involving direct client contact satisfying. Other processes to build a career upon include: solving problems, analysing data, designing images, or managing people.

However, turning the love of a product or a process into a career is not always an easy task. Some of the career applications from your interests are more subtle than others. Often, you have to dig a bit to determine both your 'true' interest as well as a viable career based upon this interest. But a career that you love is well worth the effort.

Three Dog Bakery

Recently, I attended a commencement ceremony for a Premier FastTrac® course for entrepreneurs, in which I serve as an instructor. Premier FastTrac® is an entrepreneurial training programme sponsored by the Entrepreneurial Education Foundation and underwritten by the Kauffman Center for Entrepreneurial Leadership at the Ewing Marion Kauffman Foundation. The commencement speakers were Premier FastTrac® alumni who founded a particular business called Three Dog Bakery – which is a bakery for *dogs*. Yes, you read that correctly. This bakery for dogs specializes in such delights as Banana Mutt Cookies, Apple Crunch Pupcakes and of course Poundcake.

At the commencement, I listened in awe as the two young entrepreneurs, Mark Beckloff and Dan Dye talked about starting their business in their kitchen with a 59-cent dog biscuit cutter. Later they moved to a retail site averaging five customers per day, to progressively larger stores and most recently to a joint venture with a world-wide chain of pet superstores, to supply wholesale products and bakeries to several hundred locations. At the last count the company has hundreds of employees, has been approved for franchises and is doing a multi-million dollar international business. Now in considering this choice of business, what do these young entrepreneurs have in common? The answer is obvious: their love of dogs.

Had the two entrepreneurs stopped 20 people on the street and told them about a dog bakery, I don't think they would have had too much positive feedback. Although your business need not be as exotic as a dog bakery, this is but one example of someone who took a love and then built a business around it.

The unhappy lawyer

A mutual friend put me in contact with a young lawyer who had recently moved to the area from out of state and was looking for a job. After a few minutes of conversation the lawyer confessed that she actually hated the practice of law and dreaded getting back into the profession. I was curious why she wanted to continue to practise law and asked her the following,

> 'If you hate law so much, why do you want to practise?'
> 'Because I have a law degree.'
> 'That doesn't mean that you have to practise. Why did you go to law school?'

'I don't know. All my uncles were lawyers. But I hate it. I just
don't know what to do.'
'Do you have any idea what you'd like to do.'
'Yes.'
'Well. What is that?'
'I'd like to open up a dance hall.'
'You've got your answer then.'
'What is that?'
'Open up a dance hall.'
'You're kidding, aren't you?'
'No.'

Of course, just because you have your answer doesn't mean that the work
is over. In many ways, the work has just begun. The primary goal of *Break
the Curve* is to help you to take your dream business and make it a reality.

Beware the influence of others

The important point of this whole process is to make this choice yourself.
Although it is wise to solicit input from others, the ultimate decision rests
with you. There are many well-meaning friends and family members who
are quick to dispense advice that could send you up the wrong alley. Be
particularly wary of any business proposition that sounds too good to be
true or is described as a 'can't miss' proposition. The truth is that
propositions miss all the time. And of course you know that things which
sound too good to be true, generally are.

Remember that no one can tell you the career you should pursue.
That is a decision that you need to make yourself.

Take the time you need

As with any important decision, take the time to review and reflect.
This might seem unbearable to the person who needs to make
something happen quickly. But it is better to invest adequate time at
the beginning to make a good decision, than rush into a bad decision.
After all, starting a business requires a considerable investment of both
time and money.

By their very nature, intuitive decisions require a calm frame of
mind and even additional time to reconsider. Sometimes it takes
considerable courage to make a career decision, particularly when your

chosen occupation is not considered to be a hot sector. Remember that the best ideas are not forced, but instead come from the subconscious.

If immediate funds are an issue, it might be preferable for you to take a job in the industry of your interest. That way you can pay the bills and learn the industry at the same time. That is one good way to determine whether or not a particular career is for you. Although you learn from every experience, the key is to keep the tuition low. Take the time up-front to review and reflect on your career decision. It is a wise investment.

Match your interests with the market

As we will discuss later in the marketing sections, your decision to choose your business should not be made in a vacuum. Your business will have to be viable in a competitive marketplace. Consequently, the choice of any business has to be made with an eye to the market. The trick is to match your interests with the market, to make your dream business work.

For example, suppose you want to open an Italian restaurant. But there are already several popular Italian restaurants in your small town. You are concerned that there might not be sufficient market for another Italian restaurant. In that case, you might want to consider opening the restaurant in another town or even opening up another type of restaurant. You might even decide to go after another segment of the dining market by opening up an Italian catering service.

The point is to match your interests with the market. Sometimes your initial idea for a business has to be reworked and shaped into a marketable concept. The more market driven that your business is, the greater the chances of success.

A helpful exercise to bear in mind when matching your interest to the market is to move beyond your comfort zone. Everyone has a comfort zone. People tend to gravitate around those things that are familiar and comfortable to them. However, choosing a business often requires that you move beyond your comfort zone. Tap into your innovation and creativity. Look at things a little differently. Don't be too tempted by the obvious or the familiar. Look for the unique angle or application of your business.

Don't become overwhelmed

This freedom of choice can be overwhelming. After all, the types of successful businesses that can be started are nearly infinite. Consumers need their needs met, their problems solved, and their lives made more convenient or efficient. Anything that offers sufficient value to the market has potential for a business. Some unique way of offering the same service is often a fertile ground for a new product or service.

Don't automatically exclude something because it could require specialized training or knowledge. Scott Cook, the founder of Intuit and its best selling financial software, Quicken, had no background in computers, but was driven to develop his product by his wife's frustration over balancing her chequebook. Ideas for a new product or service are around you every day. The key is to pay attention. They don't necessarily have to be totally unique or completely different. Quite conversely, ideas that are too novel require considerable time to penetrate the market and be accepted by the consuming public.

Sources of information

Although we will delve more deeply into the market research process in Chapter Five, the public library is always a useful place to start browsing for information on potential businesses. Research a topic that you are interested in. Skim through editions of popular magazines on entrepreneurship such as *Inc*, *Business Week*, *The Wall Street Journal*, *Entrepreneur*, *The Economist* and *Fortune*. Speaking of new industries, the Internet is perhaps the ultimate search tool. You can literally search potential businesses all over the world, find out about associations or even log on to chat rooms. There are also trade groups or associations for almost every conceivable product or service.

If you are interested in a certain industry, consider attending a trade show or exhibition. Often these large meetings can provide a fountain of ideas about viable businesses in your industry of choice. Manufacturers need distributors and suppliers. A business located away from your area could be viable in your area.

Congruence with your personality

Your career has to also match your personality. Don't go into the retail industry if you don't like working with people. Don't open a restaurant, if you want your weekends to yourself. In short, choose a career that is compatible with your lifestyle and personality. You know your likes and dislikes and your personal tastes. Fashion your career around these. The goal in choosing a business is to give you the best chance possible to succeed. Finding a business that you enjoy and that fits in with your personality is a definite advantage.

Don't over complicate things

If you really are at a loss as to what to do, there are also various tests administered by placement officers and counsellors that can measure your career interests. However, sometimes it's not wise to be overly analytical, since choosing a career goal is a simple process. A few years ago, I questioned my choice as a small business and tax attorney and wanted to decide what my 'real' interest was. I went to a professional counsellor and took a battery of tests to assess my career interest. The counsellor carefully reviewed my test results and rendered a professional opinion that I was best suited to be (SURPRISE!) a small business and tax attorney. In retrospect, this should have been obvious, since for some strange reason, I was always attracted to business and the law. Perhaps a short vacation to reflect could have been a better use of my time and money.

It's not really a complicated decision, the choice of a business, so don't over complicate things.

Suppose you're totally stuck

If you are really stuck on choosing a business, there are whole books written on the subject. One that I have found to be particularly helpful is entitled *Doing What You Should Love: The Ultimate Key to Personal Happiness and Financial Freedom* by Dr. Robert Anthony. Another one is *What Color is Your Parachute?* by Richard Nelson Bolles. Although the perennial best-seller by Bolles is actually geared to job seekers, there are useful exercises to determine possible interests and careers within the book.

Summary

1   It is important to choose a business or profession that fulfils your unique purpose or passion in life. It is much easier to succeed at something you enjoy.

2   Determine your choice of business yourself after careful thought and reflection.

3   Love either the product or the process.

4   Match your interest to the market.

5   Find a business is that is congruent with your personality and interests.

Action steps

- Get in a relaxed place, preferably alone or in a relaxed setting.

- Clear your mind. For a moment forget about everything that you think you should do.

- Remember that there are no rules, just let your ideas flow.

- Ask yourself the following questions:

    (a) If I could do anything in the world, what would it be?

    (b) What career would I choose if I had no risk of failure?

    (c) How could I make this a viable business? (Note: We will look more deeply at market research in Chapter 5.)

CHAPTER THREE

Building your infrastructure – finding the right people

> No man is an island. No man stands alone.
>
> (John Donne)

No entrepreneur is an island

Borrowing the famous saying above from John Donne, no entrepreneur is an island either. Many entrepreneurs picture themselves as fiercely independent. In some cases, they have forsaken an organizational structure to do their own thing. However, the entrepreneur does not have to pursue their endeavour alone and should think in terms of surrounding themselves with a team of advisers.

These advisers come in many forms. They include professional advisers, such as attorneys or accountants, who help with the technical side of the business on a fee basis. But they can also include key vendors, business associates or even customers, who also have a stake in your business. Finally, the group also includes your friends, relatives, or an informal support group who believe in your business and who could serve as your Board of Advisers.

Those entrepreneurs who are successful have generally found a way to enlist the support of others to advance their business. Your team of advisers forms the 'management' section of your business plan. But at this point you might be thinking:

> But I'm just getting started. How can I afford professional advisers?

When some think of professional advisers, they envision pricey professionals who could literally drown their business with exorbitant fees. However, with some conscientious shopping and objectives, the business owner can assemble a team that will provide the best professional

FIGURE 3.1   No entrepreneur is an island

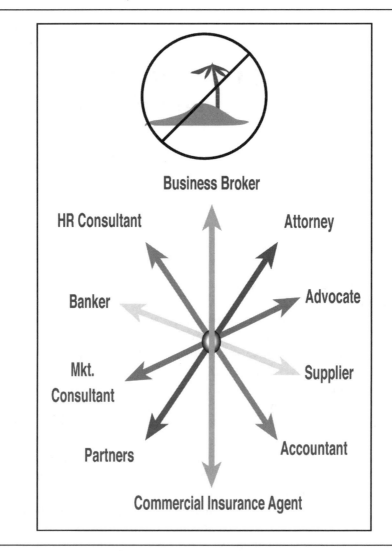

guidance at the most competitive price. In addition, you might also be able to leverage your professionals to advance your business. Not only do you profit from their professional advice, but you also might be able to benefit from their reputation and contact base. I will discuss this concept of leveraging your professionals later.

Professional advisers

The intricacies involved of running a business are very serious. Business and tax laws and other regulatory requirements have grown increasingly complex. Although money is often a scarce resource for the startup, time can be an even *scarcer* resource. During the early stages of the business, the entrepreneur is going to be stretched thin and be required to perform countless activities. Does the entrepreneur really have the time to learn how to be their own attorney ? Wouldn't it be better to pay a reasonable fee for competent legal assistance rather than form a corporation themselves with some how-to manual? The answer to this question is of course – YES. It is better for the business startup to retain the proper professional advice. The main professional advisers for the small business includes the attorney, accountant, and commercial insurance agent. In addition, the business greatly benefits from the services of outside consultants such as a marketing consultant, human resources consultant and others.

Hiring your attorney

At the risk of incurring the wrath of my fellow attorneys, I'm going to let you in on a little secret. There are a lot of attorneys in this world, particularly in the United States. In fact, I've seen legal rates actually decrease with the oversupply. So as a consumer of legal services, you can benefit by getting the most return on your dollar expended on legal services. Although the attorney market may not be as favourable in your area, the suggestions presented for hiring the best attorney at the best price will still be applicable.

Most attorneys are constantly scouring the landscape for new business. A promising business startup (particularly a well-planned effort like yours) could present an enticing prospect. Many attorneys, including myself, are willing to give a billing break to a new business in exchange for that client's loyalty and the possibility of collecting even greater fees in the future.

But obtaining a favourable price is not the only consideration in hiring an attorney. You need the services of a competent *business* attorney, one who can adequately fulfil your needs as your business grows. Be aware that there are many types of attorney in the market and some general practitioners market themselves as business attorneys when that is only a fraction of their business. You want someone whose primary focus is business law.

Some tips in hiring your attorney are as follows:

- Ask around. Ask for referrals from your friends and associates who are in business. Contact the trade association for your type of business and see who represents its members. Call the local bar association to find the names of attorneys who specialize in business.

- Once you have located a few prospects, contact them about representing you. Ask for references. Do not hire any attorney who will not talk to you (at least by phone) or an attorney that you do not feel comfortable with.

- If you are new in business or have limited resources, request a possible discount in initial fees in exchange for the potential prospect of long-term representation. If you don't ask, you won't receive. Even enquire about a possible trade out of your product or service for legal representation. Stress that this is for initial legal services only and not for the duration of your relationship. If you are sincere in both your need for a discount as well as your commitment to the attorney, you might just obtain the right attorney at the right price.

  Even if your resources are not limited, always ask about fees. If you give the impression that you are not concerned about legal fees, then your attorney won't be particularly concerned either. Enquire about the attorney's hourly rate and always obtain a flat price if you can. Many items, such as formation of a business entity, are characteristically done for a flat fee. Be reasonable, though, in your price negotiations. Your goal is not to obtain the best possible price, but rather a competitive price for a good work product.

- Respect your attorney's time, particularly if you have requested a discount. Realize that your attorney's time is their product. Only call your attorney when you really need to talk to them. When you do call your attorney, have all of the relevant facts at your disposal. Don't send your attorney off scurrying for information that you can easily find yourself. If your particular question is involved, write it down and then e-mail or fax it, along with any relevant documents. Reducing your questions to writing gives your attorney something to refer to as well as serving to flush out all of the useful information. It sometimes surprises me in my practice how reluctant some people are to commit questions to writing. They would rather waste several phone calls (and billable time) in providing the necessary information. Anything you do to make your attorney's life easier will help your relationship and maybe even your fees.

Learn to anticipate deadlines: There's nothing more imposing on a professional than having to do something at the last minute, particularly when the crisis could have been avoided. Although emergencies happen to everyone, learn to anticipate deadlines and allot your attorney the necessary time to complete the needed task.

- Size of the law firm. Law firms come in all shapes and sizes, ranging from the solo practice to international firms with hundreds of attorneys. Generally speaking, the larger firms cater to larger businesses. Since the larger firms generally have more overhead, they are usually more expensive and might not be particularly interested in representing a startup (particularly on a discounted basis). However, some of their younger associates might be more aggressive in trying to build up their clientele. The larger firms naturally have a *broader* range of personnel than the smaller firms. However, the smaller firms can have just as *deep* a talent base, particularly in a speciality practice area such as business law.

  During my 15 years practising law, I have worked at a small law firm, a medium-sized law firm and served as a corporate attorney to a Fortune 500 company, which hired some of the largest and most prestigious law firms in the world. I have concluded that there are few absolutes with regards to the size of the firm and the practice of law. I have met and worked with some outstanding (and some not so outstanding) attorneys at firms of all sizes. Since I began practising, technology has had a tremendous impact on the law. It has proved to be a great equalizer in providing ready and inexpensive access to information regardless of the size of the firm. The important thing is to find an attorney with whom you feel comfortable. That person should have the necessary talent and be able to commit sufficient time to attend to the legal needs of your business.

Hiring an accountant

Pardon the pun, but your accountant can also be an important asset to your business. Much of the same discussion above with respect to selection and fees of attorneys also applies to your accountant. Like the legal profession, the accounting industry is very competitive. Generally, your accountant should be an important business adviser, in addition to performing your bookkeeping and tax services.

Some tips for hiring the right accountant are as follows:

- Enquire about prospective accountants. Ask for referrals from your friends and associates who are in business. Contact the trade association for your type of business. Call the accounting association to find the names of accountants who specialize in your business. Interview prospective accountants also and ask for referrals.

- Hire your accountant as a business adviser. As a small business owner, you need a broad scope of accounting and management advisory services, beyond traditional tax, audit and accounting services. Ideally, your accountant would be able to function as your in-house Chief Financial Officer (CFO) to handle the wide realm of financial and management needs facing your business. In addition to having your financial statements and tax returns prepared, your business needs assistance in key financial management aspects, including startup expenses, pricing strategy, financial statement analysis, cost reduction programmes, budgeting and cash flow.

  Raising adequate funds is another big hurdle for the startup or small business. Your accountant could provide assistance by being familiar with the various sources of financing (particularly any external governmental sources) and assisting in obtaining the financing.

- Look for an accountant with experience in your particular industry. That way the accountant is more familiar with the financial subtleties of your industry and its important financial profile.

- Organize your information for your accountant. Remember that your accountant is not the financial organizer of your business. Delivering receipts and records to your accountant in a shoebox could end up giving the accountant a big headache and you a big bill. With the advent of bookkeeping software, there is virtually no reason why you can't do much of the bookkeeping yourself and use your accountant for more strategic business and tax planning.

- Tax planning doesn't occur when you submit your returns. Good tax planning occurs in the year before you send in your return. Allow the time to sit down with your accountant and properly plan your tax strategy.

- Respect your accountant's time also. Like the attorney, the accountant is highly trained and charges for their time.

- Size of accounting firm: The variation in size of accounting firms is even more dramatic than in law. There are international accounting firms with thousands of professionals as well as solo practices. Like law, while the larger accounting firms have a broader personnel base, there can be considerable talent in the smaller firms. Again, you want to choose an accountant who you feel comfortable with and who can give you the proper attention and expertise.

Banker

Your banker can also be a very important financial adviser to your business. Your business should cultivate a good banking relationship as soon as possible. In fact, it is wise to initiate a relationship before you *need* to borrow money or before you are even *able* to borrow money. In Chapter 14, we will discuss banking relationships in more detail. Be aware that banking relationships can be very frustrating to the small business. The reason is that banks are generally not risk takers and small businesses (particularly startups) are inherently risky. Therefore, the banks are not going to lend the startup any money without more than adequate cash flow and collateral, which the small business may or may not have. But it never hurts to ask. If the bank will not lend you any money now, what level of cash flow or asset coverage will they require? Often, a good banker will sit down with you and carefully analyse your projected or actual financial statements. This can lead to very valuable advice, even if your loan request is not accepted. Bankers are very familiar with cash-flow needs and operations of the business. They are skilled at spotting potential problems and may even be familiar with the financial subtleties of your business. In addition, a banker may have suggestions about alternative financing sources, including government loan guarantees. They can also serve as a sobering check to balance out the entrepreneur's natural enthusiasm. So seek to establish a relationship with a banker. If they are not ready to lend money now, keep plugging away at both your business and your relationship. You might be able to establish a commercial banking relationship sooner than you think.

Commercial insurance agent

Unlike the attorney or the accountant, the commercial insurance agent is generally paid on a commission basis for the insurance you purchase. But don't let this fact undermine your respect for commercial agents. Business insurance has its own set of subtleties and complexity. Unfortunately, today's litigation explosion has the potential to affect everyone. There's no shortage of legal theories and attorneys to advance those theories in trying to burden your business with litigation. If not properly insured, a lawsuit could prove catastrophic for your business. Therefore, a good commercial insurance agent will be able to assess your risk of loss and provide insurance that is tightly drafted to meet those risks. This has the effect of protecting you from a catastrophic loss at the most reasonable charge.

Be sure that you discuss your various risks thoroughly with your agent and that all of the necessary terms of your coverage are provided *in writing*. I know of a video producer who nearly went out of business after losing two major pieces of equipment while filming off site. Even though his policy noted that 50 per cent of his filming was done off site, his insurance coverage was limited to within 100 feet of his business. As a result, the insurance covered only a fraction of his loss.

In selecting a commercial insurance agent, look for any professional designations that are awarded to agents. Be aware that insurance companies generally charge higher rates for business coverage and work with your agent to provide them with as much information as possible about the business to help reduce rates. This information might include experience in the business, prior work experience in your field and any information about yourself that is relevant to the business. Enquire specifically about 'Business Owners' Policies,' which are speciality products designed for small businesses and which generally provide extremely broad coverage.

One good way to find the proper insurance agent is to contact them through any trade association of which you might be a member. Note that since it generally takes some time to bind insurance coverage, give yourself adequate time to obtain the coverage.

Marketing consultant

Getting clients through the door is the life blood of any business. A good marketing consultant can be a tremendous help, sometimes at a very reasonable fee. The first 'marketing consultant' that I ever used was my commercial printer. He provided excellent marketing advice regarding my materials at essentially no charge, since his printing prices were very competitive. A good commercial printer might be the first place to start in assembling your promotional materials, as many are very adept at layout and design. Other uses of a marketing consultant include designing your logo and preparing a co-ordinated marketing campaign. As with any type of consultant, be sure to check their references as well as samples of their work.

In addition, a whole new industry of marketing consultants is springing up around the infant industry of the Internet. If you are serious about using the Internet with your business, you might want to hire someone to design your home page. Examining the work of a web designer is relatively easy if you are online already. When I was preparing my Web page I received three quotations for rates. The charges for this service can be very reasonable also. Internet marketing will be discussed in more detail in Chapter Seven.

Like the other professionals, the larger and more established public relations firm usually charge a higher rate. However, often you are able to find freelance consultants who can do good work at a reasonable rate.

Human resources consultant

As your business grows and you begin to hire employees, it is important to have someone to consult about human resource matters. Keeping and motivating good employees is important to every business and an effective human resources consultant can be a very important asset in this area.

Business broker

A business broker can be an invaluable adviser for those entrepreneurs who either want to buy or sell a business. In Chapter Sixteen, we will discuss the issues involved in buying or selling a business.

Leverage your advisers

Often the advisers that you employ bring more into the business relationship than their professional skills. Each of your advisers has their reputation in the community as well as their own base of contacts. If you develop a good relationship with them, you may be able to benefit from their professional standing and contacts. I refer to this process as leveraging your advisers.

FIGURE 3.2 Leverage your advisers

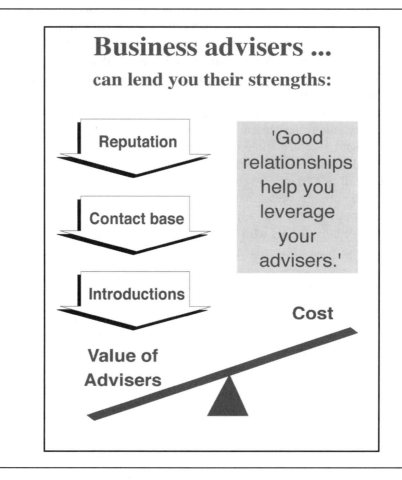

For example, your attorney might be able to refer you to their banker. The fact that the attorney has good standing in the community could favourably predispose the banker towards you. This is an example of leveraging your professional contacts. Your accountant might be able to assist you with financing also and help you present your loan request. Any of your advisers could provide introductions or referrals.

Of course, a host of caveats apply. Since providing an introduction or referral essentially amounts to a favour, you would want to establish a relationship first. You also need to exercise discretion in asking for referrals or introductions. None of your professionals are obligated to assist you outside the confines of their professional duties. Just because you've hired them does not mean that you have complete access to their Rolodex. So be selective with what you ask.

In my case, I have helped some of my clients find capital from both lenders and equity investors. But I did this only after I was comfortable with them. It is no coincidence that every client whom I helped find money had prepared a good business plan. In addition, I have also selectively provided introductions and referrals for clients.

If you think that one of your professionals can help you raise money or do some business, ask for assistance. But do so selectively.

Sometimes the leverage of a professional is based upon superior performance. Always be on the lookout for that professional adviser who can provide assistance far beyond their cost. My own speaking and seminar training career was assisted dramatically by Claire Wicker, who prepares my PowerPoint presentations. Although I tried to learn Power-Point for a number of years, I could never get past anything other than a quite ordinary presentation. One day, while attending a seminar I came across a PowerPoint presentation that was quite extraordinary. I enquired about the author and soon engaged her to prepare a presentation for an upcoming seminar of mine. She did outstanding work for a very reasonable fee at the time, since she was trying to break into the business. Based on the expected revenues from the programme, it would not have been feasible to pay the going price for the presentation. However, she made the accommodation to get my long-term business and that is exactly what happened. I use her frequently and credit her with a lot of my success in the speaking industry.

Depending upon your business, there are professionals who can add much more than their costs. This added value is another thing that you consider in leveraging.

The real key to leveraging your professionals is to find people who will give above and beyond their professional obligation. They provide you encouragement and support. Most of all, they are not working with you just for the money. They are working with you because they care. They have become your advocates.

Board of Advisers

Your Board of Advisers comprises not only your professional advisers but also your family, friends, suppliers and even some clients. In short, anyone who is interested in you or your business should serve on your Board of Advisers. Now this is not the type of board that meets regularly. Your Board of Advisers is more of an informal arrangement and actually doesn't have to meet at all. But you need to stay in contact with them on a regular basis and keep them informed about your business. That way they are in a position to send you referrals. Bounce ideas off your members. However, do respect their time and you might want to send out periodic communications. That way they can contact you if they feel like talking.

Your Board of Advisers can be a key component in your business infrastructure, if you take the time to cultivate them and communicate with them. Often a short note or announcement will do.

Partners

Another way of getting someone else directly involved in your business is to enter into a partnership with them. Sometimes people combine their skills, particularly complementary skills, and join forces in their entrepreneurial endeavour.

However, the decision to join forces should not to be taken lightly. Whenever you enter into a business arrangement with someone else, it should be treated with almost the same scrutiny as entering into a marriage. Although an engagement is not necessary, a short period of working together informally can help with your evaluation. Often people go into business together without the slightest consideration of whether their perspective partner is suitable for them or not.

Like the laws governing marriage, the laws governing partnerships impose reciprocal rights and obligations. Just like a soured marriage, a partnership gone bad can often be difficult to get out of. Consequently, if you do decide to partner up, be sure to consult an attorney, *your* attorney, to address the relevant legal issues. We will discuss partnerships and other legal forms of business entities in Chapter Eight.

Summary

1   No entrepreneur is an island. Resolve to surround yourself with the right people in the form of professional advisers and associates.

2   Take time to go through the proper steps to hire the right attorney and accountant. Your banker and commercial insurance agent are also very important. Consider other consultants in the areas of marketing, human resources, etc.

3   Find professional advisers who will work with you in the area of fees. Don't be hesitant to negotiate the best fee arrangement with your professional advisers. However, in exchange for their consideration be loyal and take the steps to make their job easier.

4   Form your informal Board of Advisers and fill it with people who are interested in your business. Communicate regularly with them and periodically request advice.

Action steps

- Follow the steps set forth in the chapters and start building your infrastructure. Begin with your professional advisers.

- Make a list of all of your contacts and friends who could serve on your Board of Advisers. Don't be bashful.

■ CHAPTER FOUR ■

The business plan – the entrepreneur's blueprint

If you fail to plan, you will plan to fail.

(Norman Vincent Peale)

The journey of a thousand miles starts with a single step.

(Chinese proverb)

The necessity of a written business plan

If you get anything out of this book, please let it be that a WRITTEN BUSINESS PLAN IS AN ABSOLUTE NECESSITY! All business owners claim to have a plan. But there are often at least two problems. The first is that the plan is only in the owner's head. The second is that the plan has not been completely worked through.

Preparing a business plan can be a time-consuming and exacting process. However, like the proverbial weight lifter, you can't get the gain without the pain. It is the discipline of sitting down and working through your plan that really forces you to confront some of the tough questions. Is there an adequate market? How much money will I need to get started? How do I handle the competition? The business plan leads you through the implications and strategies of successfully running your business.

I've mentioned before that I currently teach the Premier FastTrac® course, which instructs entrepreneurs on the preparation of a business plan. I also counsel individual clients on their business plans. I can personally attest that they're all tremendously better off as business owners for taking the time to write their plan. The primary focus of this book is to guide you, step-by-step, through the preparation of your business plan. Although the task might appear overwhelming at first, the key to accomplishing any large job is to break it up into separate pieces. That is the way that we will approach the preparation of your business plan. In the

FIGURE 4.1   The business plan: an absolute necessity

following chapters, we will focus on the various parts of the plan and I will also provide examples of a business plan in progress for your reference.

I will tell you what I tell my clients and students. You have a capability to prepare an excellent business plan. Simply follow the steps set forth in this book and you will take that large step towards fulfilling your dream of entrepreneurial success.

The benefits of goal setting

One of the advantages of a business plan is that it taps into the power of goal setting. Goal setting focuses your attention and energy on where you want your business to go. The mind can be a funny thing. You do tend to accomplish what you think about most. If you dwell on your obstacles and the possibility of failure in your business, than sadly, that is where you're apt to end up. However, if you focus on the goals and objectives for your business, you are directing your energy in a positive direction. Your business plan is your comprehensive set of goals for your business. You are charting your roadmap, your entrepreneur's blueprint for success.

I will save you the trouble of reading the myriad books in the area of goal setting and summarize for you their general contents. In order to be valid, goals need to be:

- written;

- specific;

- measurable;

- achievable.

Written

The fact that the business plan is in writing is very significant. Committing anything to paper is the first major step towards its accomplishment.

Specific

Being specific is the hallmark of the business plan. There is a saying that the devil is often in the details. Details are the foundation of any business and the same applies to yours. The items that you really agonize over constitute some of the most profound use of a business plan. The details that cause you trouble with your plan are likely to be the same details that will cause you trouble in your business. However, the main difference is that you've taken the time to carefully analyse these matters.

Measurable

Good business plans set forth financial results that are measurable. We will discuss the methods of preparing pro forma financial projections in Chapter Eleven. After you have made projections, your financial results can be measured on a regular basis. This allows you to assess your results and make appropriate changes, if necessary.

Achievable

The final requirement of goal setting is that the goals be achievable. Unrealistic estimates can quickly sink any business or quickly discourage the business owner. The business plan needs to be realistic and therefore achievable.

The business plan is a dynamic document

Although the business plan follows a general format, think of it as a *dynamic* document. In one sense, your business plan is a vibrant document which should reflect the same enthusiasm that you have for your business. Use the business plan to set forth the vision and purpose of your business. In another sense, the business plan is dynamic because it changes. Your business plan is your working blueprint. It will often change as your insights and results change. It is not something to be written and then disregarded.

Business plan software

I am frequently asked about business planning software. Although there are some good business planning software packages on the market, I still think that it is better to prepare your own business plan. Although some of the software packages can enhance the business plan with their catchy graphics, you want the plan to be an expression of YOUR purpose and vision. Outside lenders and investors can recognize this slick look and question whether the entrepreneur did the necessary research or merely filled in the blanks.

In fact, this exact issue was the subject of an article by Norm Brodsky in the February 1998 edition of *Inc.* magazine entitled 'Due Diligence'. In the article, Brodsky, a veteran entrepreneur, commented on the elaborate artwork, charts and graphs in some of the business plans that he'd been reviewing lately. One plan in particular had a very impressive presentation, but a seriously flawed analysis. As it turned out, the plan had been written by someone with little business experience who merely filled in the blanks with totally unrealistic financials. Brodsky concluded that you are setting yourself up for failure if you do a fancy plan for investors before doing a simple plan for yourself.

The plain business plan that is carefully worked out is much more beneficial than one with simple visual appeal. Although graphics can add a lot of lustre to your proposal, you must first do the underlying work. Naturally, a computer can be very helpful, particularly a word processing and spreadsheet program. Actually, many of the commercial business plan software programs are really nothing more than a spreadsheet combined with templates and canned text. In addition, many of the word processing programs like the Microsoft products already contain an integration feature with word processing and spreadsheets as well as graphic capabilities.

Although it is possible to use paper and pencil, I would urge everyone who is really serious about business to become computer literate. Computers are just too inexpensive and user friendly to have to do without them. I will address getting 'Powered Up' in Chapter 18.

Uses of a business plan

As mentioned before, your primary audience for your business plan is YOU! The business plan is designed to be your working document, your blueprint for success. I have tried to keep the business planning process as simple as possible so that you can prepare a plan that makes sense to you and which can be used in your business. Although you want to prepare your plan as professionally as possible, don't worry about impressing people. If you put the necessary time and effort into the plan, people will be impressed.

Elements of a business plan

Executive Summary (statement of purpose)

Although the Executive Summary is the shortest part of the business plan, it is certainly one of the most important parts. In addition, it is the part of the plan that is probably rewritten the most. The Executive Summary provides an overview of the business, which would include the product or service that you produce and the market that you serve. Feel free to elaborate on your statement of purpose for the business and describe your *vision* for your business.

For example, you might want to be one of the premier developers of computer games for children. Or you might want to have the best Chinese restaurant in your town. Or you might want to stress a

FIGURE 4.2   The elements of a business plan

humanitarian issue: '. . . it is our purpose to help ease the burdens of being a working parent by providing affordable child care.' Don't be afraid to set lofty goals. But be prepared to back up your claims in the body of your plan.

Management and organization

We spoke at length in Chapter 3 about putting together your business infrastructure and team members. The management and organization section of the business plan is the portion where you would discuss your professional advisers and associates.

In this section, you would also discuss the legal form of your business. We will review the various forms of business organizations in Chapter 8. This section would also be the appropriate place to discuss any prevailing legal issues that could impact your organization. This would include any pending litigation or intellectual property issues.

Description of the product/service

This part would contain a more detailed description of the purpose of your product or service. The key is to emphasize the *unique* features of your product or service. Elaborate on the benefits of your goods and services from your customers' perspective. You could also mention the history of the product or service and any spinoff or related products or services.

Also include a profile of the industry in which you will be operating. The industry profile would include a discussion of the size of your market, the type of market and your growth potential. Next would be a competitive analysis of similar products and services. Remember that competition is a way of life in the business world. So you need to have a good understanding of the competition. Compare yourself with your competitors on the basis of factors such as price, quality, selection, additional services and facilities or locations. That exercise will further help you understand and define the nature of your competition and then determine what your competitive advantage is. In Chapter 5, we will review market research and the competitive matrix profile.

Marketing plan

The marketing plan begins with a discussion of your customer profile. Who is your customer? What is your target market? The key element of a successful marketing plan is to know your customers – their likes, dislikes, expectations. By identifying these factors, you can develop a marketing strategy that will allow you to arouse and fulfil their needs. Targeting your market is centred around identifying customers by their age, sex, income, educational level and residence. As we will discuss in Chapter 6, businesses that succeed usually do not try to be all things to all people. They carefully segment the market into one or more target areas at which to direct their marketing efforts.

Next would be a discussion of the marketing mix and the promotional strategies that you will use to reach your target market. Chapter 7 will present the basics of the marketing mix, which are the product, place, price and promotion. The product or service that you offer is naturally one of the most important parts of the marketing mix. In the description of the product or service above, the unique aspects of your product or service were emphasized. Now, your marketing plan needs to capitalize on those unique aspects in promoting your product or service to your target market. Since your marketing dollars are finite, focus on those promotional techniques, such as print advertising, media, public relations, the Internet, which best advertise your message. Another important part of your marketing mix is your pricing strategy as well as your distribution strategy. In Chapter 7, we will examine the factors involved in the preparation of your marketing strategy.

Financial data

The entrepreneur needs to first estimate their initial capital requirements, which are the resources necessary to get their business up and running. Next would be the projection of operating results. These activities would involve the accounting tools of the start up budget, pro forma cash flow statements and balance sheets. Chapters 10 to 12 will discuss the accounting and financial components of the business plan.

The financial data is the glue that holds the rest of the plan together. The financing sources for your business are discussed in this part of the plan. You can finance your business with either debt or equity or a combination of both. Chapter 13 will discuss the advantages and disadvantages of debt and equity. Chapter 14 will present some advanced financing strategies such as private placements and public offerings.

Conclusions

End your business plan with a bang. If you are using the plan to raise money, take the opportunity to demonstrate why you think that your plan will be successful. Show confidence in your business and in yourself by ending your plan on a positive note.

Appendices

The appendix would contain such items as product literature, articles about the business, personal resumé, relevant research, or anything that you feel is relevant to the business. As a question of format, I favour a business plan in the 30-page range which is focused on the presentation of the topics listed above. All other relevant matter can be placed in the appendix. That way the 'meat' of the business plan is more easily accessible.

You always win with a business plan!

As I stated earlier, the business plan is the best place to articulate the goals and aspirations for your business. According to the statistics compiled by the Entrepreneurial Education Foundation, the vast majority of people who successfully complete the Premier FastTrac® course *and* prepare their business plan ultimately succeed. This is a dramatic reversal of previous estimates of small business failure. Entrepreneurs claim that they are too busy to write a plan. Everyone is busy. But those who make the time, reap the rewards. In today's fast-paced economy, there is simply not time for everything. There is probably no situation more pressured than running a business. The demands on the small business owner are almost infinite. Without careful planning, you run the risk of being distracted from the higher payoff activities.

Proper planning helps take advantage of what has come to be known as the 80/20 rule. According to the 80/20 rule, fully 80 per cent of your results come from 20 per cent of your activities. For example, you generally make 80 per cent of your revenues from 20 per cent of your customers. You receive 80 per cent of your complaints from 20 per cent of your customers. On a personal note, you wear 20 per cent of your clothes, 80 per cent of the time and so on. The point is that as a business owner you want to devote the majority of your time to the higher payoff activities, that 20 per cent that produces 80 per cent of your results. Planning is certainly one of them. The added benefit of planning is that it will direct you towards higher payoff activities.

I'll share with you a little writer's secret, which can help you prepare your business plan. This secret is called the first draft. Every writer knows that the best way to keep their writing moving along is to get that first draft down and then revise it. Word processing has made this very easy. Do the same with your business plan. As you get ideas, either jot them down or start typing. Then revise later. The point is to get started, since that really focuses you. Some of the material comes very easy while other material will take some time. If you feel that you're stuck, keep moving. Perhaps reread something that you don't understand and then try to complete that part of the plan. Go back and revise later. As I mentioned earlier, the business plan is a dynamic and not a static document. Expect it to change as your insights change. But you've got to start somewhere. Set a deadline for preparing the first draft and resolve to meet it. It is amazing how focused and motivated we become as the deadline draws near.

A recent experience best illustrates one of the main benefits of writing a business plan. A local university sponsored a business plan writing competition in connection with a public programme on entrepreneurship. The rules were simple. Submit a business plan on a prospective or existing business. The plans would be judged and those submitting one of the five best business plans would be invited to lunch with Victor Kiam, the owner of Remington Products. If you haven't heard of him, Mr Kiam is an extremely successful entrepreneur and his book, *Going for It*, is an inspiring tale of entrepreneurial success. Consequently, the opportunity to obtain some first-hand advice from an entrepreneur as successful as Victor Kiam, was an enticing prospect.

A friend of mine heard about the contest and asked for my advice. He was considering starting an independent publishing company. Although time was relatively short, I urged him to prepare a business plan and gave him some materials to help. My friend quickly put together a business plan by the competition deadline. Although far from perfect, I felt that his plan was fairly good, particularly in light of the time pressure. And as it turned out, my friend won a spot for lunch with Mr Kiam. But the most interesting part is that my friend won because *only five people ended up submitting written business plans*. Although many had called about the contest, only five had taken the trouble to prepare a *written* business plan. To me, this anecdote illustrates the following moral: YOU ALWAYS WIN WHEN YOU WRITE A BUSINESS PLAN. The main reason for this is that so few of your competitors take the time.

Summary

1 A written business plan is essential for all businesses.

2 Your business plan is a dynamic document, which reflects your unique purpose and vision.

3   The main sections of the business plan are the Cover Page, Table of Contents, Executive Summary (Statement of Purpose), Description of the Product or Service, Marketing Plan, Financial Data and the Appendix.

4   In writing your plan, focus on completing your rough draft and then revise it. Remember that the business plan is a dynamic document and meant to be revised along with your insights.

5   When you prepare a business plan, you always win!

Action steps

- One of the best ways to get started preparing your business plan is to get started. So right now either write down or go to your computer and type the Cover Page and the Table of Contents page for your business plan. Alternatively, you may want to write it out in a notebook or a legal pad. Put the title of your business on the Cover page. Then, on the Table of Contents page, list all of the parts of the business plan: Executive Summary (Statement of Purpose), Description of the Product or Service, Marketing Plan, Financial Data and the Appendix. Then, list all of the major parts of the business plan at the top of separate sheets of paper. Congratulations! Now you've got the outline of your business plan. You have taken a step that fewer than one in 20 business owners take.

- Now write out the Executive Summary section of your business plan. What is going to be the overriding purpose or vision of your business? What products or services will you offer? Into what markets? Remember that the key is to get something down and revise later.

PART II

Preparing the business plan

■ CHAPTER FIVE ■

Marketing research – investigating your business concept

Genius is one per cent inspiration and ninety-nine
per cent perspiration

(Thomas Alva Edison)

Overview of market research

Once you have chosen your business concept, your next step is to research and investigate it. It is important to carefully analyse the feasibility and the market for your business. Although choosing your business comes from the inside out, working out the details is resolved from the outside in. In other words, while you are free to choose the *type* of business that you want, its particulars need to be fashioned by the marketplace.

In Chapter 2, we discussed matching your interests with the market. The purpose of the market research is to further refine that sense of direction into a successful concept. This isn't about changing direction, but rather is more about focusing and tweaking your business. Today's rapidly changing economy is extremely market driven. Consumers are growing more particular for services and ideas that provide value and make their lives easier. By researching and paying careful attention to the marketplace, you will be able to transform your business concept into a successful enterprise.

A few caveats before we begin market research are outlined below.

Don't get overwhelmed!

As we will see, the sources of data and information, particularly in the online world, is nearly infinite. Consequently, it is very easy for the first time or even the regular researcher to become overwhelmed. It will be helpful to get an overview of the information first before venturing into details and making conclusions. Depending on how many concentrated blocks of time you can devote to your market research, expect to spend several days to a few weeks gathering and analysing information in order to refine your business concept. Set time to do the research into segments and then go after it. If you don't have the time, you can hire an expert to do your market research. But it must be done, whether you do it yourself or hire a researcher. It is an investment that you simply can't afford not to make.

If you follow the tools of the book, research can be made as painless as possible. Sometimes you will feel like you're spinning your wheels to extract those golden nuggets. But they are there and if you look for them in a systematic fashion, you will find them.

Begin with the end in mind

When you start your research, begin with the end in mind. Keep in mind the types of concepts that you are interested in and look for items relevant to your business concept. Expect that you will also uncover the unexpected and that your research path may change depending upon what you may find. Follow the new information because it may cause you to change your mind about how you're going to handle your marketing or your operations.

Enjoy it!

This might be a stretch, but looking up things can be fun if you let it. In the entrepreneurship classes that I teach, some of the loudest groans come in the market research section. Outside research often reminds people of the unpleasant memories of scurrying around school libraries looking for information on their term papers. I know that I thought school was difficult enough without the burdens of outside research. But on the other hand, try to appreciate the research process, knowing that some valuable piece of information could make the whole search worthwhile and could even contain the seeds of the next Microsoft. You'll find that as you uncover certain facts, light bulbs will go off in your head and your ideas will begin to flow. Also learn to appreciate the value that research brings. Research reduces the risks of making bad decisions and increases the chances of making solid business decisions that will affect just how successful your business will be.

Make the reference librarian your best friend

Obtaining the assistance of a good research librarian can dramatically decrease your learning curve and at least get you started on the right foot. However, some important things to remember are that you can't expect the librarian to do your research for you and you need to be courteous in asking them for assistance. Their job is to point out or suggest sources, not to actually look anything up.

Learn to analyse and interpret the data

Since it is rare that you're going to find exactly what you need, learn to read between the data and interpret it. The technical term for this process of reading between the lines is interpolation. Remember, that unlike major companies, your research budget and your time are limited. Sometimes you're simply going to have to do the best that you can with what you have. Marketing can be considered a blend between art and science. Often, there are no exact answers, and even the large companies with their enormous resources have to make some educated guesses. Sometimes my entrepreneurship students become frustrated because they cannot find the exact data that they need. But the key is to get a feel for the market through your own fact gathering and what others have gathered and written and be able to make educated judgment calls.

Understand marketing

This is related to interpreting the data. Although marketing is often thought to be the 'soft' academic discipline in business schools, it can actually be very quantitative. In addition to the disciplines of finance and accounting, marketing is an unusual blend of information and data as well as intuition and instinct. Your goal in this chapter and in the chapters that follow is to get an instinct for researching and marketing your business.

For example, marketing research for a retail coffee shop would be very different from that of an international business consulting service. For a retail coffee shop, geography and location would be very important. Unless the coffee shop decided to ship products out of the area, its market would be fairly defined. An initial reference source for a coffee shop might be the phone book and an automobile as opposed to the reference books that will be described below. The business consultant would naturally be more mobile in their client base and accordingly would need a vaster scope of research in their industry in different geographic areas. The point is to develop an instinct for these differences.

General research strategy

There are three main areas or components that you will need to research:

1   your particular industry;

2   the market (consumers and their buying decisions);

3   the competition.

One overriding goal behind your market research is to determine your market potential. During this research process, an overriding question should remain in the forefront of your mind. This question is whether or not there is a market for your product or service. If so, how much? Is there room in the present market? Are there gaps in the market? What you are looking for are opportunities in the market to position your product or service against the others. Therefore, you want to obtain an understanding of the industry in which you will be trying to position yourself. Next is the subtleties of the market for your goods and services. What are the consumer preferences in your industry? In addition, you want to have a thorough understanding of your competitors so that you can analyse where the market opportunities might lie.

Industry

The first place to begin in any market research project is to seek out information on your particular industry. It is important to get an overall feel of the type of industry that you working in, understand its market niches and determine where you fit in. You want to be able to make an assessment of the condition of the industry. For example, is the industry in a declining or an advancing position? Is it already saturated with competitors? As an added complication, the condition of the industry may differ depending on the geographic location and related events. The health of the industry in your area may be different from that on a national or global level.

When looking at your particular industry, it is important to assess it against global trends. For example, more and more of the population

FIGURE 5.1   Overview of general research strategy

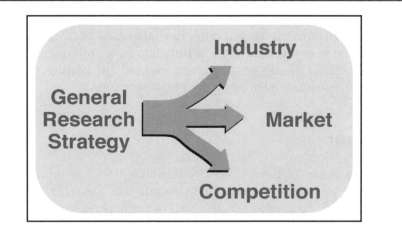

bulge of those born after World War II are reaching retirement. What will this mean to your industry in particular? In researching the industry, you also want to understand the major players or products and services in the industry as well as understand its dynamics.

After you obtain an overall feel for your industry, the next step would be to focus your analysis on particulars of the industry as they relate to your particular situation. Get an understanding of the consumers and the trends in your industry. What are things that leading businesses are doing that are successful in the industry? By dividing the industry into its component parts, you are looking for the interaction of the industry with suppliers, with its affiliates or related entities.

Consumer market

After you have generally researched the industry, you need to turn your focus on the consumer market, and in particular, your market. Now you are focusing on your customers and information about a defined geographic area. Learn as much about your desired market as you can. Understanding them ('getting close to the customer') will give you a competitive edge by understanding what your customers might value in the business and services of your industry.

Such information may seem overly detailed for now, but all of this research and information is directed at understanding the consumer and the market. It is often the subtleties of the industry where the real opportunities lie.

Large companies spend enormous sums trying to determine customer preference. Since you don't have that kind of money, research is very essential in this area. Later in this chapter, we will discuss manual research, which can be an important method in locating published research on consumer preferences and lifestyle profiles.

Competition

The third area for you to focus on is your competition. It is important that you analyse what you do in relation to your market. You want to compare yourself to your competitors on the basis of as many relevant variables as possible that affect customer decisions. There are several questions to consider when analysing your competition. Who are your five nearest direct competitors? Who are your indirect competitors? What is the condition of their business: Steady? Increasing? Decreasing? What are their strengths and weaknesses? How does their product or service differ from yours? These would include price, quality, selection, customer service, facilities, and location.

One way to organize all of this information is on a competitive matrix profile, which appears as Figure 5.2 Although the competitive matrix profile may constitute a considerable amount of work, it will pay extremely valuable dividends in deciding how to tailor your business to the marketplace.

Sources of research

Information comes in two basic categories: primary and secondary. Primary data is new information that is being collected for the first time. Think of the word: primary. It takes measurements from a new point in time, or from a new point of view, or from a different set of sources from before. For example, the United States census compiles primary research every 10 years. Primary information includes statistics compiled by the government, or information gathering agencies. For the business, primary information also includes your competitive matrix profile as well as interviews with your customers who frequent businesses similar to yours. Statistics are usually derived from primary research and are often the raw data from which you can directly derive some conclusions.

FIGURE 5.2 Competitive matrix analysis

Competitive factor	Business 1	Business 2	Business 3	Business 4
Direct or indirect competitor				
Price				
Quantity				
Selection				
Additional services				
Business conditions (steady, increasing, decreasing)				
Strength/weakness				
Facilities/locations				

Primary data can also include information derived from interviews with consultants, personnel in companies and associations, friends inside your business, friends outside your business, the grapevine, and suppliers. Never forget the customer as the most valuable source of information.

Secondary information is information which already exists and which also could have been compiled and filtered from various sources. An example of this is newspaper stories. Secondary information includes books, government studies, and information gleaned from online services and the Internet. Secondary information exists in tremendous quantities and at a great variety of levels. Often it will supply you with most of what you need to know. It's usually yours for the taking – *if* you have the time and *if* you can find it. When using information from secondary sources do be attuned to potential biases and know that it can contain errors. The best way to guard against misleading information is to find the same information in a separate source. It is the goal of the information researcher to ascertain as much primary and secondary information as possible that applies to their product or service.

The three methods of research

There are three basic methods you will use to conduct your market research:

■   manual;

■   telephone research;

■   electronic research.

Manual research

You may be tempted to jump right on the Internet, but this is not always your best starting point. Begin with the reference section of your main public library (branches usually do not have the quantity of resources). If you have a university library nearby, it is probably designated as a community library and it will also be open to the public. It will have a great depth and breadth of resources as well. Starting with manual research will give you a good overview of what's available and provide leads to other research sources. Eventually, you will be able to walk over to the computer terminals there and use those, but we will get to that in a moment.

Start with the reference librarian and tell this person what your goal is and what you are looking for. They will suggest multiple sources. Use the database to look up books written on starting up and/or operating a business like the one you are interested in. Check them out if possible. Next, check the *Encyclopedia of Associations*, and the *Small Business Source Book*. If these publications are not in your area, ask the librarian about similar reference materials. Each will give you more sources such as contact information for trade associations, industry data and references to articles and trade publications. Take a look at *CACI's Lifestyle and Market Analysis* or another consumer market analysis. It will provide market profiles, lifestyle profiles, demographic segment profiles. It also lists information on post codes based on the latest census and figured with growth estimation. Another item included is an index by activity (for example, gardening, travel). If the library does not have CACI's, see if they have any type of demographic profile information.

While in the library, it is also useful to search for information about your industry in the various business periodicals. There are numerous periodicals on particular industries, which contain pertinent information about 'war stories' in the industry. Articles are sometimes written by other members of the industry as well as consultants. Often flipping through the periodicals will give you much useful information about your particular industry.

Check your local newspaper archives for articles on your particular business. They may be indexed and microfilmed or it could be available electronically. You can then make copies of the articles from the microfilm or print it from the terminal.

Telephone research

If your local newspaper is not available electronically or on microfilm, you can try to get any articles via the telephone. Call your local paper and see if they have an internal library and if you can get copies of articles that way.

Now that you have conducted your manual research, you have a list of associations for your particular industry. Call them. Ask for the library or public information department. Ask for any materials they can send you concerning your industry.

Also from your research, you should have uncovered the names of some individuals who have knowledge about your business. Call them and interview them. Be prepared with your questions, however, and make use of their limited and precious time. Before you get off the phone ask if they think there is anyone you should speak to regarding your subject. Send a thank-you note if they were helpful.

Your telephone research will also include your competitive research which you can conduct by phone. Your starting source is the local telephone directory.

Electronic research

On your second trip to the library, you now have a clearer focus on which to rely for your electronic research. See if your library has any CD ROM databases that contain either bibliographic references to or full text of articles from various magazines, newspapers, or newsletters. One example that your library might have is the ABI Information or Periodicals Index. Again, ask the reference librarian for guidance if you are unfamiliar with these sources. Conduct keyword searches or use their indices.

At this time, you are also ready to go on the Internet and see what there is, not only in terms of basic information, but also to see Web sites of other similar businesses. Notice how they present their business. Expand on others' good ideas, but respect their copyrighted material.

Although a new area of law, copyright laws are being applied to this new electronic medium. Maintain your focus and stay on the paths that pertain directly to what you need to know.

If all of this research seems overwhelming, don't be alarmed. That's natural. Remember, you can always hire someone to conduct the research for you. It can be done for a reasonable amount of money. But whether you do it yourself or hire it out, it must be done. Otherwise you are making your business decisions in the dark.

To illustrate some of the principles of this book, I will periodically reference by example the entrepreneurial endeavours of a young couple named Kathryn and Jean Paul. Jean Paul is from France and Kathryn is from New York City. The two met in New York City, where they were both working in the hospitality industry, and later married. Shortly afterwards, they travelled to New Orleans to attend the International Jazz and Heritage Festival. They fell in love with New Orleans and decide to move down and open up a bed & breakfast called the Chateau Orleans. Although the data and analysis used in their business planning process is meant to be as authentic as possible, Jean Paul and Kathryn are fictitious and not meant to indicate any suggested age or profile of an entrepreneur. Their successful story could well be yours.

Now back to Kathryn and Jean Paul. Both are in their mid 30s and have never owned a business before. Kathryn has worked in the hotel industry for several years, primarily in the areas of guest services and customer relations, and is currently working for a large hotel. Jean Paul has also worked in the hotel and the restaurant industry, and is currently working as a waiter at a restaurant in the French Quarter. They live in the Garden District area and would like their B&B to be located there.

Although the two have diligently pursued their own careers, they have never opened a business of their own. They have combined savings of approximately $45,000 and considerable energy and ambition to succeed. However, they do want to be prudent and intend to carefully study their options and prepare a business plan before plunging in.

Following the action steps recommended in this book, Kathryn and Jean Paul begin asking around to find competent professional assistance. They begin to assemble their various advisers. They also prepare their Executive Summary. At this point their goal is to open a distinctive and profitable bed & breakfast in the Garden District of New Orleans, the Chateau Orleans. Their next step is to research the bed & breakfast industry.

One afternoon before his evening shift, Jean Paul pays a visit to the downtown public library. He requests assistance from the reference librarian about materials on the lodging industry in general and the bed & breakfast industry in particular. She looks up some items in the database and directs him to several books written on starting up a B&B. She also directs Jean Paul to several journals on the B&B industry. In the *Encyclopedia of Associations*, Jean Paul finds listings of associations in the travelling, lodging and bed & breakfast industry. He makes a note to contact them and obtain some recent material on the industry. Jean Paul becomes so immersed in his research that he is almost late for work. He later makes several more trips to the library, sometimes joined by Kathryn. Material starts arriving in the mail. They find more articles and then log onto the Internet to check out several on-line sources of information on the B&B and travel industry, as well as web sites for existing B&Bs.

Within a short time, the two become very knowledgeable about the B&B industry. Their research determines that the lodging industry is in a strong growth position. In particular, small inns have experienced considerable growth, growing from a few thousand in 1980 to over 25,000 properties by 1997. The small inn category consists of three categories:

- home stays: private homes where one to three rooms are made available to guests,

- bed and breakfast: commercial lodging endeavours with five to ten rooms, and

- the country inn: full service lodging facility with 10 to 20 rooms.

In addition, nearly two thirds of all inns contain between five and 12 rooms. According to industry statistics, the average annual revenue of a seven-room inn is $146,045 or $20,720 per room. Jean Paul and Kathryn obtain a recent survey from the Professional Association of Innkeepers on the bed & breakfast industry.

This data assisted them tremendously in refining their business concept. Although they had initially planned a six-room inn, perhaps there were better opportunities with a larger B&B.

TABLE 5.1   Bed & breakfast industry analysis

Number of rooms	Total revenue per room	Total expenses	Net income (1)
1	$10,261	$13,897	($3,636)
2	5,984	7,715	(1,732)
3	8,680	8,646	34
4	12,304	9,191	3,113
5	16,070	10,628	5,442
6	15,719	10,870	4,849
7	16,473	10,791	5,683
8	15,926	8,303	7,623
9	18,662	12,681	5,981
10	20,678	12,386	8,292
11	28,060	18,481	9,578
12	27,911	20,142	7,770

(1) Income before deducting Mortgage, Depreciation, Owner's Draw and Income Taxes. Excerpted from the Professional Association of Inkeepers International's Fifth Biennial Industry Study of Bed-and-Breakfast/Country Inns 1996 Operations, Marketing and Finances, P.O. Box 90710, Santa Barbara, CA 93190. 805/669-1853.

With a clear understanding of the national industry, their next step was to determine a competitive matrix analysis for their inn based on the local competition. They discovered that New Orleans contained many B&Bs and went ahead with painstaking research to prepare a competitive matrix analysis. Playing the role of shopper, this exercise took considerable time in phoning the various B&Bs for information as well as obtaining brochures and information from the Internet, as some of the B&Bs had web sites. When they had finished, they had over 40 entries of information in table format similar to that shown in Figure 5.3.

By completing the competitive matrix analysis, Kathryn and Jean Paul were able to know what their competition is offering in terms of rates, services and amenities. They also obtained a jump start on their marketing plan by determining where the various B&Bs advertised. Other items of interest included whether the rooms have private baths or not, what kind of breakfast is served, what amenities they offer, what credit cards they take, etc.

FIGURE 5.3 Chateau Orleans' competitive matrix analysis

B&B address/ phone	Source see key below (1)	# of rooms	Rates	Private bath	Bfst (2)	Parking	Amenities (3)
1	BK	9	95-105	All	C	On	P/T/K
2	TD/B	11	75-101	2	C	On Off	P/T
3	TD/WS	14	95-130	All	C	Some	P/T/K/A/B
4	BK	12	76-126	All	C+	On	T/A
5	WS/TD	15	70	1	No	2bks/$	T/P
6	TC	12	65-125	All	No	On	P/T/A
7	WS/TD	9	60-115	All	No	Some	P/T/C/K
8	H	14	200+	All	F	On	J/B/E/AL/F

(1) Source Abbreviations
  TD = Telephone directory
  B = B&B information provided from the B&B itself.
  H = Hotel information provided from the hotel itself.
  I = Inn information provided from the inn itself.
  TC = Tourist commission
  BK = Books
  WS = Web site

(2) Breakfast
  C = Continental
  C+ = Continental plus
  F = Full

(3) Amenities
  P = Phone
  T = TV
  K = Kitchen
  O = Pool
  J = Jacuzzi/whirlpool
  A = Antiques
  R = Restaurant
  E = Evening cocktails/wine/hors d'œuvres/tea
  B = Balconies
  C = Courtyard
  G = Fitness
  N = Newspaper
  AL = Airport limo
  F = Fireplaces
  V = VCR

Needless to say that after completing the above competitive matrix analysis for over 40 properties in their area, Kathryn and Jean Paul had a good idea of the competition in their market. Their next step was to engage in market analysis and define their target market, which is the next chapter in this book.

Summary

1   Market research is important to investigate your business concept.

2   Use a concentrated strategy to gather market data that includes understanding the industry, the market, and your competition. The purpose of market research is to further refine your product or service into a viable business based upon the realities of the market.

3   Use both primary and secondary sources of research to gather information.

4   Three methods to conduct market research include manual, telephone and electronic research.

5   After you've researched the industry, prepare a competitive matrix analysis on your market.

Action steps

- Research the industry that you are interested in. Prepare an overview of the industry, its market and your competition.

- Use primary and secondary sources of research to gather information.

- Prepare a competitive matrix analysis of your competition.

- Revise your product or service, if necessary.

CHAPTER SIX

Marketing analysis – defining your target market

Every situation, properly perceived, becomes an opportunity.

(Helen Shucman)

After researching your industry, the next decision is to define your target market. In this competitive era, the businesses that survive and prosper are not those that go after everyone, but rather those that strategically target their market. A new business often makes the mistake of thinking that they are for everyone. But remember that one size does not fit all and it's not a good strategy to try to be all things to all people. A preferable strategy is to select one or more target markets and to pursue that market.

In deciding to focus on your market, don't be concerned about the business that you might leave behind. You don't have to focus on an enormous potential market to be profitable. The truth is that there's plenty of market share to go around even in the most competitive of environments and in the most competitive industries. However, if you take the time to target or segment your market, you will be able to distinguish yourself from the competition.

Even on a large scale, there are many cases of companies that tried to be all things to all people and failed miserably. These companies lost sight of their mission and their purpose. Failing to focus is not only a poor marketing strategy, but a poor operational strategy as well. One popular management buzzword of the last few years has been 'core competency.' Simply put, core competency means that companies should focus on what they do best. A decision to target your business might be closely related to your 'core competency' because you're making a decision to focus on a segment of the market that you can best compete in.

There are examples of targeting the market all around us. Targeting in the personal services field is known as specialization. It is no mystery that the higher earners in such fields as medicine or law are those professionals who specialize. They become known in the marketplace for their specialized services and are therefore able to command a premium.

Targeting can be very important to your business. While it might serve to remove some of your customer base, it can also serve to remove your competition. It is much easier to attract business when you are the proverbial big fish in a small pond rather than the opposite. Targeting applies to practically every industry, from the retail to professional services to manufacturing and distribution. The decision to target or segment a certain part of the market is based upon the same principles and thought processes as choosing a business in the first place. The only difference is that you are now choosing a part of the original market.

Targeting analysis might make the new business owner a little leery. The startup who is scratching for customers is not particularly enamoured at the thought of turning anyone away at the door. I am certainly not recommending that you do this. Many new business owners make a decision to specialize when starting out. But they still accept business not related directly to their target markets, because it helps pay the bills in the beginning. Sometimes the new business has to work into their specialization strategy from a more general position. Targeting can be something that you do decide on from the start or something that you ease into gradually.

For example, suppose you open a retail clothing store. You could decide to target men or women, teenage women or the upscale market. If you open a print job shop then you might target other businesses, rather than individuals. This does not mean that you'll ignore others, but rather will focus on advertising in your target market.

Targeting your customer – developing a customer profile

The first idea when deciding on a target market is to choose the type of customer that you wish to focus on. Since all marketing is ultimately driven by the consumer, think about or visualize the customer that you would like to serve and be most comfortable serving. Are your customers young or old, male or female, very affluent, other businesses or people with families?

It is important to really get to KNOW YOUR CUSTOMERS. What are the needs of your customers? What type of problems or issues are your customers trying to solve? What are their likes and dislikes relative to your particular product or service? If you can figure this out, then you

FIGURE 6.1   Developing your customer profile: know your customer

have conquered an important hurdle in your business. Figuring out what your customers want and giving it to them is the heart of all marketing. Marketing is most effective if it responds to the needs and the likes of the customers. Your job, to the extent that you can accomplish it, is to try to get into the hearts and minds of your target customer.

The American company Frito Lay has a massive marketing department designed to understand the people who consume its potato chip products. Since potato chips are not generally items of necessity, it is extremely important that the company knows their customer. At an outside research facility, the consumption patterns of its customers are studied very carefully. The company knows the size, weight and texture of the chips that are preferred by their customer and the entire company is very market driven. Obviously, few businesses have the resources that Frito Lay does to gather information at this level and precision.

Hopefully, you have been able to gather some valuable customer information based upon your research activities outlined in the previous chapter. Now is the time to review your research and determine your customer profile. This would include a profile of your ideal customer, and all of the various characteristics of the target audience.

Once you identify the characteristics of your target audience, the next step is to identify segments or groups with similar needs and wants so that you can appropriately target your marketing to them.

This process of targeting your market is known as segmenting the market, or niching. The techniques that will be described regarding this process are very similar to those used by the large companies. If carefully followed, these techniques could greatly assist in developing your unique position in the marketplace.

Market segmentation – finding your market niche

Market segmentation involves breaking down a large heterogeneous market into smaller markets or segments. It consists of making the decision to view the market as one that comprises of many smaller parts. The strategy is to provide a product or products for each different segment that fits and maximizes the total market. However, for market segmentation to be successful, your business needs to look for a pattern of similarities where consumer preferences form distinct clusters.

FIGURE 6.2 Market segmentation

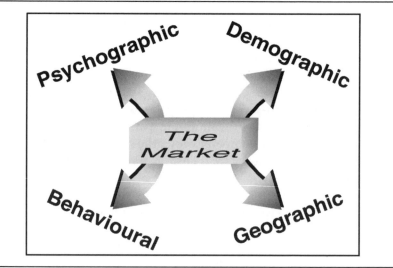

There are a number of bases for market segmentation:

- *Demographic.* Demographic factors are one of the most common forms of market segmentation, primarily because the factors are relatively easy to measure. Demographic factors include age, sex, income, marital status, occupation, education and nationality.

- *Geographic.* Segmentation on the basis of geographic factors is based upon where people live. Geographic factors could include (a) large city vs. small town, (b) cold vs. warm, (c) eastern vs. western and (d) northern vs. southern.

- *Psychographic.* The basis of psychographic segmentation is people's lifestyles and their personality. Factors include their activities, interests and psychological profiles. For example, are they conservative or risk-taking, outgoing or withdrawn, compulsive, ambitious, etc.

- *Behavioural.* These factors divide people up by various behaviours, such as their usage of particular goods and services, purchase occasion, brand loyalty and responsiveness to price and promotion.

Don't get alarmed if this seems a little complicated, because market segmentation can be somewhat involved. I am not suggesting that you have to segment your market with all of the above factors. Depending upon the type of customer, some of the factors listed above will be much more important for purposes of market segmentation. The key for you is to pay attention to your customers so you can understand how best to target them. A market segmentation analysis involves the following steps.

Determine market boundaries

It is very important that you define the market that's going to be served. Remember that you can't be all things to all people. Pick a part of the market that you wish to serve. This could be based on input from your competitive matrix profile. Based on the competition, what part of the market are you going after?

Decide which segmentation variables to use

Go through all of the variables to decide which are most likely to be useful. Are you going to focus on women or men? Younger people or older people? Those with families or single? Those who are studious or those who are gregarious? What variables make sense given your business? The primary market that my law practice is geared to is new and growing companies. My clients tend to be both men and women in their 30s and 40s, who are intelligent and highly motivated. One psychographic characteristic about them is that they are all results oriented. Consequently, they like their legal work done quickly and reliably. Therefore, I focus mostly on anticipating their needs and providing efficient legal service.

Collect and analyse segmentation data

Some of this data can be gathered during the research steps used in the previous chapter. Perhaps you might want to gather this data yourself through informal interview or even a short questionnaire to existing or potential prospects. Determine which segments appear the most alike. Although this might appear to be a cumbersome process, the type of targeting that results from a good segmentation practice is certainly worth the effort.

Develop a profile of each segment

Although it is wise to go after one segment at a time so that you can concentrate your efforts, you might want to develop a profile on more than one segment. The segment profile will contain your all-important customer profile.

For example, your men's clothing store might be targeted to professional men between the ages of 30 and 55 who earn in the top two per cent of the income or $80,000 and who regularly spend $750 for suits. Your customers tend to be conservative and serious, who are very status conscious and want their clothes to provide them with a professional image.

Target the segments to be served

Decide which segment you intend to pursue.

Design a marketing plan

We will address this in the next chapter.

Working with your market niche

One key thing to remember is that this segmentation or niching process is not something that you do once and are finished with. Quite the contrary, finding and working with your niche market is a continual process for your company. To begin with, your niche has to be aggressively marketed to your target customers. Promoting your niche would need to be an important part of your marketing plan. In addition to promoting your niche, it would also be necessary to continually reevaluate and refocus your market niche.

Remember that a good market niching strategy begins with a preliminary focus on a desired part of the market. Market niches do not come to you. You have to go after them. You need to constantly be on the lookout for all of the subtleties related to your market niche. Remember that the bottom line behind market segmentation in the first place is to determine buyer behaviour.

Always take the opportunity to survey your customers, either through a questionnaire or informally regarding their preferences and desires. Sometimes business publications contain survey results that could cause the light bulbs to go off in your head. Once you are in business, you will have the advantage of being able to survey your customers. Their responses will give you further insight into what drives their buying behaviour. You will need to do this constantly as buyer behaviour changes with some frequency. Another type of informal research with your target market is to ask them for the speciality items that they really want.

One successful example of surveying buyer behaviour concerned a repair business which later became a very successful motor oil change franchise. In doing a survey, the owners found that the majority of people having their oil changed were women. These women were actually intimidated by the service station personnel who, in many cases, they perceived as too dirty to work on their car. The franchise capitalized on this in designing a clean facility and providing amenities such as coffee and a pleasant waiting room.

Test your niche

As discussed above, the successful market niche is based upon what is going on in the heads of customers. If your niche does not distinguish you from your competitors, then it is not going to generally be a successful niche to follow. After you have established your niche, the next step is to test market your product or service to determine whether your customers and/or organizations recognize that they are special services. Try to get clients in the door to sample your product or service and get their feedback. Test your product or service to determine whether there is a positive reaction. Depending on your resources, you can give the clients a questionnaire to really see what their reaction is.

Remember that one of the advantages of a niche is that you can really eliminate the competition. Once you find a tightly defined niche market you can position yourself within the market, and dominate your niche. That would be another way to determine whether you are succeeding with your niche strategy. Dominating your niche should be the focus of your niching strategy. For example, you can pinpoint the associations and publications of your target market.

Behind every niche is a talent or particular interest that you have. It is no accident when you see professionals specializing in something about which they happen to be enthusiasts. For example, a sports attorney I know is a die hard sports fan. The niche came as second nature to him. Some of us are lucky enough to stumble upon particular niches in our business. In other cases we have to go and create the niche. The important thing is that we know our customers and understand their behaviour and then determine what they are all about.

Your evaluation of niching strategies is closely related to the Executive Summary of your business plan. Your niching strategy goes back to the picture of what your business basically is. Decide how your business will stand out with particular customers.

Another important strategy in identifying a niche is to look to see where its trend might be. Once you have actually selected the niche strategy, the next step is to decide to employ a marketing strategy that exploits the niche. The key is to position yourself so that you are constantly in the minds of your target consumer and much of your selling is done by them or they advocate you. Once you decide to niche, the marketing effort must be aggressive and ongoing. One way to do this is to conduct seminars. Newsletters are also a good marketing tool. One way to concentrate on getting free media coverage is to make a list of the publications and find out who the editors are. Call them and identify yourself as a contact with a reliable source of sound information.

After considerable market research, Kathryn and Jean Paul begin to generate useful ideas about targeting their bed & breakfast. The segment of the travel market that they intend to focus on are the younger tourists, primarily international. This is a market that they already know and would feel comfortable serving. While these younger tourists are budget minded, they can afford and will pay rates on the economy end of the B&B industry. Through their research at the convention bureau, Kathryn and Jean Paul have determined that although the younger traveller comprises a significant portion of the New Orleans tourist market, they are not marketed to by many segments of the travel industry. Most of their competitors in the Garden District area focused on more upscale older travellers. In fact, Kathryn called several existing B&B owners, who told her that they often turned away some of the younger travellers, primarily because of price considerations.

Other research done by Kathryn and Jean Paul included contacting several local travel agencies. They posed questions regarding the type of accommodation that international tourists were looking for. They also mailed short questionnaires to the travel agencies as well as the consulates of several European countries that were located in New Orleans. The two even spent a few weekends at Jackson Square in the heart of the French Quarter surveying tourists and determining their needs. All of their research consistently revealed a shortage of acceptable economy accommodation for the international traveller.

A customer profile began taking shape. Their targeted customers were in their 20s or 30s, college educated, who enjoyed travelling for entertainment as well as cultural reasons. Although this clientele was not particularly affluent, they generally had good taste and were conscientious price shoppers. They were generally looking for no frills accommodation which was clean and acceptable. Many were students or recent graduates.

At the end of this detailed but fun process, Kathryn and Jean Paul were excited. There was an important niche market in the travel industry right under their very nose. Out of the millions of visitors who come to New Orleans annually, they were going to focus on perhaps one of the more overlooked segments, which did not constitute part of the convention industry or an affluent travel base. In addition, Kathryn and Jean Paul felt drawn to this market. As young travellers themselves, they understood the difficulties of travelling on a budget. They understood the economy traveller who wanted clean, basic accommodation, but might not mind communal facilities such as bathrooms. These types of travellers were seldom in their rooms so the amenities offered on site were not a major concern. What the travellers valued were a close proximity to the area attractions and particularly the thought of being around other younger travellers. They understood that those people travelling from out of the country sometimes had problems with the language. Kathryn spoke some Spanish and Jean Paul was fluent in German, in addition to French and English. Other subtleties for this target market included a less restrictive policy for serving meals. Most of the other B&Bs served meals at a particular time. However, with the younger travellers more drawn to the night life, an early sit down breakfast the next day was not of particular concern. They were perfectly content with generally having a self-serve breakfast available to them.

Making the decision to focus on this part of the market at the inception of the venture was very important. Kathryn and Jean Paul realized that they were going to need a larger building than they had initially thought. In addition, the building would be renovated more in a dormitory style with some shared bathrooms.

Summary

1   Your business cannot be all things to all people. Target a particular market and then pursue it.

2   The essence of marketing is to *know your customer*. Although you don't have the sophisticated research tools of large companies, there are many ways that smaller businesses can also use to get to know their customers.

3   Part of the targeting process includes segmenting your market on the basis of demographic, geographic, psychographic or behavioural

characteristics. Decide which market segments or niche markets to pursue.

4   Periodically test and refocus your market niches.

Action steps

- Select a preliminary focus or target market for your business.

- Develop a customer profile of your ideal customer. What are their likes, dislikes, etc?

- Segment the market of your business into its various target markets on the basis of the most relevant variables, e.g. demographic, etc.

- Gather and analyse any segment data that you have.

- Establish your market segments or niche markets.

CHAPTER SEVEN

Developing your marketing plan

Progress always involves risk. You can't steal second base and keep your foot on first.

(Frederick Wilcox)

In the previous two chapters we have discussed the two basic principles of marketing, which include marketing research and defining your target market. We also discussed the competitive matrix profile and the importance of assessing yourself against other competitors in the marketplace when you were beginning to formulate your marketing strategy. Remember again that your strategy here is to be unique, against both your target market as well as your competitors'. In the previous chapters, we discussed the importance of identifying the target market, determining the needs and wants of your customers, and to detailing your product or business as tightly is possible to those anticipated needs. In addition, it is also important that you become intimately familiar with your market and the type of customer to whom you plan to market.

The final step in your marketing strategy is marketing management, which is the actual formulation of a marketing plan. Your marketing plan will involve the juggling of the marketing mix and the promotional strategies that you will use to reach your target market. Your marketing strategy represents the culmination of your research and implementation into an action plan. Included in this discussion of a marketing plan are some low-cost marketing strategies and the brave new frontier of marketing on the Internet.

Fundamentals of your marketing mix

The traditional marketing mix includes the following:

FIGURE 7.1   Fundamentals of your marketing mix

1   Product or service – the most important part of the marketing mix is the product or service that you will offer to your customers.

2   Price – generally the price is the cost of product to the customer.

3   Place – involves the location of your business as well as your distribution strategy. This involves such decisions as how to hold inventory or transport goods.

4   Promotion strategies – these strategies are generally the most visible to consumers. The promotional strategies describe all of the sales and marketing communications, including public relations, personal sales, and promotion and advertising. It's everything used to help make the consumer public aware of your product or service.

Product or service

The importance of your product or service cannot be overestimated. The uniqueness of your product or service is an integral part of your marketing mix. You want to be able to emphasize the uniqueness of your product by differentiating it from other products. Such differentiation includes the packaging and the features of the particular product.

Hopefully, the competitive matrix profile that you completed earlier yielded important insights into positioning your product to differentiate it from the others. The term 'unique selling proposition' (USP) is often used to depict what is unique about your particular product or service. Every business needs to determine its USP. In addition, your business has to be able to communicate the USP to the marketplace. This is particularly true for a segmented or niche market.

Pricing strategy

Your pricing strategy is another area that is very important to your business and which can dramatically affect your overall competitiveness. As we will see, there is a reason why your pricing strategy is in a marketing chapter as opposed to an accounting chapter. That is because the price for your goods should be *market* driven, as opposed to being *cost* driven. The pricing strategy for your business is more involved than simply a cost plus strategy, which would be to take your costs of production and add a margin. However, using only a cost plus strategy is often a quick way to go out of business because it results in the underpricing of your goods. Although the cost does figure into a pricing strategy, it should not be the only factor or even the starting point for setting the price.

Your pricing strategy is determined by the marketplace. One good way to determine the market price is based on the competitive matrix profile that you completed in the earlier chapters. In addition, the pricing decision will also be co-ordinated with the type of marketing strategy that you will use. A complete price strategy involves determining a reasonable range of prices that take into account the *price floor*, the *market price* and the *ceiling price* and based on a competitive analysis of the following three factors.

Price floor

The first place to start in pricing your goods is to figure a price floor. In figuring what your price floor is, you need to be sure to include all elements of your cost, including material costs, labour costs and overhead costs. Sometimes it is helpful to perform a break-even analysis to determine your break-even point.

Market price

This is also known as the 'going rate' which might tend to vary depending upon the pricing of similar goods in your area. Note that the perceived quality is important in setting the price. Depending upon your target customer, your pricing in this case is very dependent upon your competitive position. Your marketing strategy could be to price at or below the competition.

Ceiling price

This would be the maximum price that could be charged for a particular good or service and is usually based upon a premium perception of a particular good or service.

Before setting the price for its goods, your business should carefully consider the above factors. As stated before, the price that is set could reflect the marketing strategy. However, the business owner should be very conscious of price sensitivity and sometimes has to change the prices to reflect the market. In Chapter 12, we will go into more detail in pricing analysis by setting out break-even points and contribution margins.

Note that the overriding strategy in pricing is to make it EASY for the customer to buy.

Place

The place involves the decision about where to sell. For the retail outlet, your location could be very significant. Once you have determined your target market and product, the next decision is where to deliver your product or service. Distribution involves the movement of products in all stages of development, from resource procurement through manufacturing and on to final sales. Note that the Internet is providing new avenues concerning places to sell goods.

Promotion strategy

Your promotion strategy is the method you use to convey the image of your product or service to the consuming public. For the startup, funds for promotional activities will be somewhat limited. However, as we will see later, it is important to budget some funds for promotion because you do need some way to get customers in the door.

To begin with, it is important that you closely co-ordinate your promotional strategy. The underlying theme that should run through all of your promotional activities is maintaining a professional image. Your print and graphic ads should focus on the image that you want to portray to your customers. Your promotional activities should converge on a single theme, possibly your USP, to reinforce your message and your products.

The following is a checklist of items that you might want to keep in mind in preparing your promotional strategy:

- My advertising expresses the numerous benefits that my clients receive when they use my services.

- I advertise to reinforce my uniqueness. I have a unique selling proposition which explains who I am.

- I know who my clients are, where they are and what benefits and features they are looking for in my kind of service.

- I have a business name, by-line, logo, business colours and company typeface that communicate who I am.

Since every business, particularly the startup, has a limit on promotional funds, you need to be extremely careful about the types of media that you select. Often those wanting to sell you media will tend to overestimate its benefits. Perhaps you might want to test different types of media.

Always look for ways that you can get free media or inexpensive media that will usually fit within your budget. For example, I wrote articles for business periodicals in exchange for print advertising. Maybe you have the opportunity to exchange goods and services for advertising where possible. Constantly be on the lookout for the best use of your advertising dollar.

Print advertising

When evaluating print advertising, you want to keep in mind your intended mission in advertising and the amount of exposure necessary to reach your market. Reach and frequency are important quantitative measurements involving media. Reach is the percentage of your target market that sees the ad and frequency is the number of exposures. Be sure that if you spend money on print advertising, it's in the publications that your target market reads.

Print advertising is generally a very effective method, but also an expensive method for the small business. Usually one ad will not suffice. Conventional marketing wisdom says that your ad has to be seen by someone seven or more times before they remember the product or service. In addition, since the space is so precious within the block of the ad, several things should be kept in mind in preparing print advertising:

- The headline – this is the primary item of importance in print advertising. In order to get a potential customer's attention, you have to literally hit them over the head. Otherwise, there is simply too much competition for the reader's eyes and attention. Graphics can also play an important role and work in conjunction with the headline.

- Subhead line or opening paragraph is also very important. Although generally much smaller than the headline, it is still very critical. While the headline might have got the attention of the prospect, this opening paragraph must keep their attention.

- Benefits – the heading and ad copy need to be loaded with benefits for a potential reader. Don't save your best material for later. Most people will continue reading only if they like what they read early in the ad.

Public relations

Public relations can be *extremely* beneficial to the small business in the form of free media or advertising. However, the business needs a strategy to obtain positive media coverage. Remember that the trade press is always looking for solutions to problems. If you can position your company or service to provide some of those solutions, you'll be able to obtain some trade press. Often, the uniqueness of your product or service determines how much trade press exposure you are likely to receive. I spoke earlier about Three Dog Bakery, which is a bakery for dogs. Naturally a business that unique had the potential for considerable trade press. In fact, it was an article in the *Wall Street Journal* that really helped to propel their business.

Although your business may not be as unique as Three Dog Bakery, be aware of the trade press that covers your particular industry. As mentioned above, they are always looking for solutions to problems for their readers. The key is to not be shy. If you think you have the answer for a particular problem, go ahead and send an article in to the trade publications. The rules generally require that you send the article to one editor at a time.

Direct mailing

Generally, direct mail is one of the least expensive, and most measurable ways to help sell products or services. Since you are sending the message directly to a particular individual or business, you can compile the particular results. Direct mailing allows for the easier tracking of the promotional message as well as the content of the message.

One way to stay in constant touch with your customers is to use direct mailing to a customer list. To begin with, request that your customers complete a preferred customer card. This would also apply to any potential customers and would allow you to keep a qualified mailing list of preferred people to whom to announce specials, promotions, changes to services, or existing services. You could also ask questions and can gather information that will help you to better target your mailings. Other ways of obtaining customer mailing lists include acquiring membership lists of local organizations, clubs and churches or copying the names and addresses from the cheques of your customers. Qualified mailing list companies that sell names can also provide lists, but usually the lists are not as good as those that you generate on your own. Remember, it is better to have several hundred qualified names than thousands of nonqualified names.

One form of direct mail which is worth special mention is newsletters. Newsletters are becoming an increasingly important source of promotional activities for any type of business. Sometimes, the use of newsletters can be combined with a web site to produce electronic newsletters. Generally, you are using a newsletter to increase the visibility of your business among a potential target base. Rather than directly promote your business, the newsletter gives you more of a 'soft' sell by highlighting some of the activities of your business and providing some useful information to the reader. Accordingly, you want your newsletters to be reader friendly and attract attention. The logo that you use in your newsletter is very important since you want to entice the reader to at least scan it. Generally, it is better to have several key points in a short newsletter, as opposed to a longer newsletter without key points. The key with newsletters is to attract interest, to increase visibility and to position yourself in the eyes of the reader as an expert in your field.

Television and radio

The use of paid advertising on both television and radio can be very useful to small businesses. However, remember that there *are* production costs associated with producing spots from either medium. The advance of cable television has provided new outlets to small businesses, as its rates are generally very affordable. In addition, the specific types of programming of cable TV (e.g. sports, music, education) provide already existing target markets to which to direct your advertising. Spots on some of the larger television networks are usually out of the reach of the budgets of small business. Radio can also be an effective advertising medium, as there are some demographic profiles of its listening base.

However, remember that the key to advertising is repetition and the small business needs to be sure that it has an adequate budget to fully utilize the media. Spending your advertising budget on a fantastic promotional spot doesn't do your business much good if you then don't have the funds to air the spot.

Advertising on the Internet

Perhaps one of the more revolutionary developments for small businesses today are the opportunities offered by the Internet and the World Wide Web. Although these tremendous resources are still in their infancy, they can still have a tremendous impact on your business. The World Wide Web can serve as the great equalizer in business, providing your company with a cyberspace storefront equal to competitors many times your size. In addition, the Web offers some of the lowest cost per exposure forms of advertising in history. Clearly, any marketing plan for small business is incomplete without at least considering the Internet and the World Wide Web.

But don't think that the Internet will relieve you from having to do the other forms of advertising discussed above. While the Internet can help your business, it is not going to handle all of the marketing duties. You have to strategically work in Web advertising with the ongoing marketing plan of your business to be effective. Don't be fooled into thinking that you can simply set up a Web site and the business will just flow in. Some businesses have done very well on the Web while others have done poorly. Success stories include catalogue companies like 1–800–FLOWERS and L.L. Bean and online superstores like Amazon.com and CDNow.

As an aside, the story of Amazon.com stands as a testament to preparing a business plan as well as utilizing the on-line world.

Amazon.com was founded by Jeff Bezos, a former Wall Street executive. After researching the market (sound familiar?) Bezos concluded that books were a commodity that could be sold online. Since an Internet bookstore could be based anywhere, Bezos decided to pack up for Colorado. While his wife drove, Bezos prepared his business plan on a laptop computer in his car. Today, Amazon.com is one of the largest sellers of books online. However, before we discuss the impact of the Internet and the World Wide Web on your business, let's be sure that we have a basic understanding of the terms.

The World Wide Web evolved from the Internet. The Internet was started by the United States Department of Defense to protect its national security information during the Cold War. Later, government institutions and educational facilities used the Internet to share information and further research. The World Wide Web started in 1993.

One of the major advances done in establishing the World Wide Web was the introduction of hypertext markup language (HTML) and multimedia. HTML served to eliminate the previously intricate Internet commands and replace them with the point and click options of HTML. This allowed the introduction of graphics and multimedia on the Internet, which opened up the World Wide Web to the general public.

The Web could certainly be used to promote your business. As stated before, the Web permits a small business to construct a multimedia, interactive site that will allow it to showcase itself to the entire world. When you compare this with the cost of printing and circulating expensive glossy advertising, it can be a bargain. You can use your web site as your brochure, to describe the services or products that you offer, provide product demonstrations and even compare yourself to your competitors. However, your decision to create a web site does involve some expense, and like all of your advertising expenses, it should be carefully considered. In addition, a web site will not necessarily guarantee a flow of customers, or any customers for that matter.

There are several steps involved in preparing your web site.

Web site construction

Your first step is to create your web site. An entire marketing industry has grown up around the construction of web sites and there is no shortage of companies or individuals that will prepare a site for you. Some of them even advertise their services on the web and offer to create sites at bargain prices. However, I would be very wary of anyone advertising these services at too competitive a rate. Remember that you get only what you pay for and the same is true when you are designing your web site. So if you don't have the necessary skill to prepare the web site yourself, you might want to hire a professional. But just like any professional adviser hired, get quotes and ask for references. One advantage of Web designers is that you can so easily inspect their work.

In designing your site, there are three factors to keep in mind:

1   content;

2   visual appeal;

3   ease of use.

The content of your web site is most important. People use the web for information which is valuable to them. Just as you target your business to customers, you also need to target the content of your web site to your customers. What would be helpful to your customers? You want to make that site informative and provide solutions to your customers' needs. Once the site is established, you want to take the time to keep the content fresh and vital for your customers.

A good site is also visually appealing. If you use pictures, make sure that they are sharp and of good quality. Don't be afraid to use graphics, but do exercise some caution. A general rule of thumb is that your site needs to open up generally in 10 seconds or better. Resist the temptation to overuse graphics and clutter your site, since your site needs to be easy to use. Make it easy for your customers to use your site and find the information, particularly information on how to get in touch with you. Be diligent in following up on all leads.

Other items in preparing your site include external links to other sites. Again, a balance must be struck between leading the reader to good information, but also ushering them out of your site. Although I recommend external links to other sites, one way to avoid running people out of yours is through 'framing', which allows the visitors to stay within your site while they visit others.

Web site posting

After design of the site, the next step is to register your site with search engines and other tools so that Web surfers can find you. Sometimes part of the service involved in designing your web site also includes posting your Web site everywhere that your present and potential customers might look for you. Posting sites on the Internet involves a lot of knowledge about the Internet itself, and not just the Web. One item that you want to negotiate with your web site developer is the proper posting of your site.

Web advertising

Despite the posting of your site in search engines, you have to be proactive in advertising your site. Just as no entrepreneur is an island, no site is an island either. Advertise your web site and work it in with your other advertising plan. Remember to list your web site on all of your other media, which would include your brochures, business cards and announcements. Take advantage of the media synergy that can be created with your traditional and Internet advertising.

Another use of the Internet is to be able to sell products directly to your consumers. Electronic commerce is every business person's dream and certainly possible for your business. A full discussion of this is beyond the scope of this book. Suffice it to say that at this very moment companies are trying to figure out how to use the Internet to sell more products or services and increase their direct commercial traffic. Doing business over the Internet is still in its infancy and requires a secure system to take credit card information or even a toll free number on which to take orders. Perhaps your site might prompt e-mail inquiries that could later be handled by your business.

As mentioned earlier, some businesses are doing very well on-line while others are not. How large a role the Internet plays in your marketing plan will be determined by your business and the manner in which the Internet evolves. However, I think that the possibilities offered by the Internet will only increase. As a small business owner, I would urge that you make a concerted effort to work the Internet into your business – now. That would help position you on the forefront of change as opposed to just following along.

Low cost narketing strategies

We are now going to take the opportunity to shift from the decidedly high-tech world of the Internet and the World Wide Web to the markedly low-tech topic of low-cost marketing strategies, which should be in the marketing plan of every small business.

Let's start with networking. Networking is one of the cheapest advertising strategies that you can do for your business. Everyone claims to network, but the key with networking is to do it constantly. Remember that the main person promoting your business is YOU! You are your own best brochure or web site and you should take advantage of every opportunity to promote your business. Be certain that everyone you know is aware of your business and what you do.

Try to establish a definite networking strategy. This would involve joining any associations and groups that could generate leads for your business. Don't just join, but become involved and volunteer for assignments. That allows people to see you in action and become impressed with your ability.

The key to your networking is the ability to communicate your business to potential customers in a way that raises their interest. Practise your 30 second 'sound bite' about what you do for a living. Describe your business in a way that shows your confidence. Say it convincingly and be comfortable with it. When people ask me what I do, I reply that I help businesses to grow, prosper and avoid paying taxes. Who could disagree with that? This is better than simply saying that I am an attorney and leave the other person to guess what I really do. Practise your sound bite in intervals of one minute, 30 seconds and 15 seconds. The key is to get your point across and make a good impression. You run into business prospects all day long. Do you take the time to inform them about your services in a way that peaks their interest?

Sometimes networking involves joining associations that you do business with in addition to the associations that you are already a member of. I'm always amazed at how some of my fellow attorneys restrict their networking to activities involving the bar association. Hanging out with other lawyers does not produce clients. You need to hang out with people who send clients to lawyers. That is why I was always very active with the accounting association. The same applies to your business. Join and become active in those associations that could serve as a referral base. When you go to meetings and functions, don't just talk with your friends. Make the effort to meet new people and let them know what you do. Set a goal of five new contacts at each function and don't leave until you've met your goal.

Recognize that, like any other marketing activity, networking and word-of-mouth marketing takes time. People generally like to do business with those whom they know and trust. Take the time to earn that trust.

Figure 7.2 presents a checklist for your marketing plan. The table lists various promotional activities and deadlines in connection with a marketing plan.

FIGURE 7.2 Marketing plan worksheet

Promotional activity	Use or not	Cost	List of activities	Timetable
Promotional material				
Brochures			1. 2.	
Stationery			1. 2.	
Announcements			1. 2.	
Business cards			1. 2.	
Logo			1. 2.	
Print advertising				
Magazine			1. 2.	
Newspaper			1. 2.	
Other				
Public relations				
Press kit			1. 2.	
Direct mail				
Newsletters (print)			1. 2.	
Mail piece			1. 2.	
Internet				
Web site			1. 2.	
Newsletters (electronic)			1. 2.	
Media				
Radio			1. 2.	
Television			1. 2.	

Jean Paul and Kathryn begin to develop their marketing plan in accordance with the schedule set out in Figure 7.2. They decide too that they need brochures and announcements for their business. They also think that a newsletter and a web site would be very important to the business. They set up a plan to develop these materials within certain deadlines and move forward with them. They establish a total budget of $5,000 to spend on their initial marketing activities. They also plan to use some direct mail and begin to target their customer base.

They also plan to network extensively. These activities include the contacting of government agencies in the New Orleans area who deal with foreign tourists. They join the Tourist and Convention Bureau and begin meeting other people in the industry. Their draft worksheet of their marketing plan is shown in Figure 7.3.

FIGURE 7.3   Chateau Orleans' marketing plan worksheet

Promotional activity	Use or not	Cost	List of activities	Timetable (from March 1st)
Promotional material				
Brochures	Yes	$2,500 including consultant	1 Hire marketing consultant 2 Prepare logo 3 Give draft of copy 4 Send to printers	1 30 days 2 45 days 3 60 days 4 75 days
Stationery	Yes	$100	1 Prepare logo 2 Send to printer	1 45 days 2 50 days
Announcements	Yes	None	1 Prepare draft 2 Circulate	1 5 days 2 15 days
Business cards	Yes	$75	1 Prepare logo 2 Send to printer	1 45 days 2 60 days

Promotional activity	Use or not	Cost	List of activities	Timetable (from March 1st)
Print advertising				
Magazine	No		1 2	
Newspaper	No		1 2	
Other	Yes	$350	1 Advertise in tourist listing	
Public relations				
Press Kit	Yes	$50	1 Mail announcement of opening to periodicals 2	1 60 days
Direct mail				
Newsletters (print)	No – next year			
Mail piece	Yes	$500	1 Send out brochure to travel agencies and foreign travel bureau 2	1 90 days
Internet				
Web site	Yes	$1000	1 Have marketing consultant prepare site at reduced fee since did other work 2	1 90 days
Newsletters (electronic)	Yes		1 Mkt consultant will design first electronic newsletter 2	1 90 days
Media				
Radio	No		1 2	
Television	No		1 2	

Summary

1   The fundamentals of the marketing mix include product or service, price, place and promotion strategies.

2   Promotional activities include print advertising, public relations, direct mailing, media and the Internet.

Action step

■   Prepare your own marketing plan worksheet.

CHAPTER EIGHT

Business and tax law basics – choosing your form of organization

Destiny is not a matter of chance, it is a matter of choice.

(Anon.)

Business and tax factors

One of the first decisions for the new business is choosing the proper form of legal organization. This decision has a tremendous impact on the business and should be made carefully. In reviewing the various legal entities and their business and operating and tax considerations, I will focus primarily on business forms of organizations in the United States and in the United Kingdom, which I think are generally applicable world-wide.

Some of the factors to consider before forming your business organization are listed below.

Tax implications

The tax implications are certainly one of the most important aspects of forming an organization. As we will see, each of the forms of business organization has a different tax structure and tax implications. Be sure that your attorney is aware of the various tax implications or has consulted with your accountant.

Owner's liability

For many, the owner's liability certainly runs a close second to tax implications (if not first). Although in the startup, many owners feel that

FIGURE 8.1   Factors in choosing a form of organization

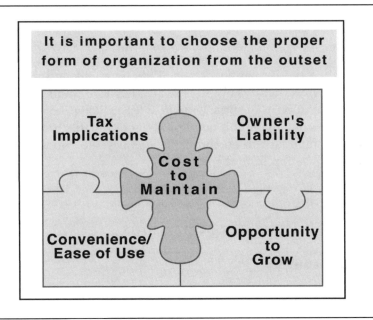

their business is their life, it doesn't have to be that way from a legal standpoint. There is no reason why the business owner needs to have more liability for the operations and debts of the business than is necessary. As we will see, some forms of business organizations allow the owner to shield their personal assets from creditors of the business.

Convenience/ease of use

Convenience of the business form should not be overlooked. Ideally, the owner wants a business organization that is flexible and serves the owner, rather than the other way around. It is not good legal strategy to form an organization just to have one.

Opportunity to grow with business

Although the type of organization should be easy to use, it should be flexible enough to grow as your business expands. Changing the form of organization in mid-stream can be expensive and disruptive. It could also trigger adverse tax consequences.

Cost to maintain

This is related to ease of use. Particularly in the start up phase of your business, you don't want to have to spend excessive costs on an organization and use up any more resources of the business than necessary.

So while the formation of organizations might be simple at first sight, we see now that it is not so. The attorney who wants to put you in the fad organization at the time without at least talking about some of the above issues is not giving this question the scrutiny that it deserves. That is why it is important to go through the issues and choose the proper form of organization from the outset.

Forms of business organizations

Sole proprietorship

Of course, the easiest thing to do when starting a new business is to do nothing. But that may not always be the wisest decision. Many small business startups decide not to form a legal business organization, and instead open their doors as sole proprietors. By doing so, the owner is essentially treating the business as an extension of themselves and accounting for its profits on their personal tax returns.

The main advantages of the sole proprietorship is its low cost, simplicity and flexibility. In fact, most business startups begin in this manner. But the sole proprietorship's main disadvantage is that it leaves the business owner with unlimited liability. Since the business is an extension of the owner's personal estate, the owner has to answer personally for its debts and obligations, including lawsuits.

Any liabilities or debts of the business would become the personal debts of the owner. With respect to business loans, this may actually be a distinction without a difference. Most lenders are going to require the owner to personally guarantee loans. Lawsuits against the business can be a different matter. As a sole proprietor, the owner is *personally* liable for any lawsuits. Although some businesses would not be considered inherently risky, even the most flimsy legal claim can pose a serious financial burden to the business owner.

Sole proprietors can address some lawsuit risk through the use of a personal liability umbrella insurance policy. This is an area that you need to discuss with your commercial insurance agent. Some of these liability policies can be purchased at a modest cost. Although it does leave the business owner with some risk, the sole proprietorship makes sense for someone who is testing the water with a new venture because it requires less tax maintenance and is easily dissolved.

Partnership

The partnership is very similar to a sole proprietorship. Entrepreneurs who are considering launching a business with someone else might consider the partnership because it is flexible and simple. But unlike the sole proprietorship, it involves the creation of a separate business entity, which is the partnership.

The tax consequences are generally the same as the sole proprietorship, with the income and losses of the partnership flowing through to the individual partners. In addition, the individual business partners do have personal liability for the debts and obligations of the partnership. This would include lawsuits against the business.

Also a word of advice for those of you who are considering going into business with someone else. As was stated before, entering into a business partnership is much like a marriage. There are reciprocal rights and obligations between the individual partners. Consequently, when entering a partnership, it is important to have partnership documents which address the various rights of the parties. The partnership agreement should address issues such as the termination of the partnership, the death or disability of a partner and the sale of partnership interests.

There is one form of partnership that does limit the liability of the partners. That is the limited partnership or the Partnership in Commendam. The limited partnership has two types of partners – the general partner and the limited partner. The general partner is very similar to a partner in a regular partnership in that they manage the entity and have unlimited liability for its debts and obligations. However, the limited partner is liable only for their share of the partnership, provided that they are not actively involved in the business. Consequently, the active business owner could not be a limited partner. However, a passive investor in the business could be a limited partner.

Corporation

Most areas of the world recognize the corporate form of doing business. Although the terminology might be slightly different, the basics of a corporation are as follows. The corporation is a separate legal entity

formed by the preparation of articles of incorporation which are filed
with applicable legal authorities of the particular jurisdiction. The articles
of incorporation generally set forth the name, business purpose, management structure and capitalization of the particular organization. In
addition to its incorporation documents, corporations are governed by a
body of corporate law which affects the rights and responsibilities of the
shareholders, officers and directors of the corporation. The corporate
form has been around for many years.

One of the main advantages of incorporating is to shield yourself
personally from the liabilities and obligations of your business. Although
some lenders will still require a personal guarantee, the corporation will
protect the owners personally from lawsuits against the business. In
addition to shielding the owner, the corporate form of organization also
serves to separate out business from personal record keeping. Separate
accounting systems and cheque books are maintained and the corporation is run as a distinct legal entity.

However, one of the main disadvantages of the corporation is its tax
treatment. Since the corporation is considered a separate organization for
both legal and tax purposes, there is a tax imposed on its profits. This tax at
the corporate level is in addition to taxes paid by the business owner on
any dividends or salary received from the business. This tax at both the
individual and corporate level is often referred to as double taxation.
Remember that both the sole proprietorship and the partnership had a
flow through tax structure which imposed tax only at the individual level.

There are other unfavourable tax consequences of the corporation.
Business losses are generally trapped at the corporate level and cannot be
used to offset other sources of income. In addition, any assets that are
distributed by the corporation to its owners could also trigger tax
consequences.

In the United States, one way to avoid this double taxation of profits
in the corporation is to choose small business treatment or become an S
corporation under the Internal Revenue Code. In making this election,
the income and losses of the corporation flow through to the individual
owners or shareholders. This has the effect of removing one level of
taxation.

Limited liability company

A new form of organization that has become popular in the United States,
the United Kingdom and other parts of the world is the limited liability
company or the LLC. One way to picture the LLC is a hybrid form of

organization that falls somewhere between the corporation and the partnership. The LLC can provide the best of both worlds, combining the limited liability of the corporation with the flow through tax consequences and single level of taxation of the partnership.

Like the corporation, the LLC is formed with Articles of Association, which is similar to Articles of Incorporation. Instead of bylaws, the LLC uses an Operating Agreement. The terminology for the LLC is a little different from that for corporations. Instead of shareholders, officers and directors, the LLC is owned by its members and run by its managers. There are certain rights and responsibilities for LLC members and certain powers and duties for the managers.

Because the LLC is fairly new, it does not have the years of case law and practice to back it up. However, it is well accepted now in the United Kingdom, the United States and other parts of the world. In fact, even the US Internal Revenue Service has officially recognized the LLC and sanctioned its tax treatment.

Generally speaking, the LLC is more flexible than the corporation. For example, there are no restrictions on financing the LLC and no rules on discrimination between classes of ownership. In addition, it is possible for a member to withdraw and receive fair market value for their interests. Another advantage to the LLC is that capital contributions by members can be made in form of an obligation to perform future services. Since the LLC is similar to a partnership, assets can be transferred in and out of the LLC on a tax free basis.

I mostly form LLCs in my practice, although I still form both corporations when there are valid tax and operating reasons. Although many of the forms for business organizations are boilerplate, I would still highly recommend that business owners consult legal and tax professionals before choosing their form of organization. Like everything in business law, there are pitfalls and subtleties, and business owners would be well served by competent professional advice.

Other considerations

There are some other factors to be considered when choosing your form of organization. These include:

- *Whether a new business or conversion of existing business*. If converting an existing business, you need to determine whether or not any tax or operating considerations of the previous business would preclude you from making the conversion.

TABLE 8.1 Forms of business organizations

Entity	Advantage	Disadvantages
Sole proprietorship:	1 Simple 2 Flexible 3 Low cost 4 Centralized management	1 Unlimited liability 2 Lack of continuity of existence
Partnership	1 Separate entity 2 Flexible 3 Simple	1 Unlimited liability 2 Lack of continuity of existence
C-corporations	1 Limited liability 2 Centralized management 3 Well known 4 Certainty in the law	1 Complex and expensive 2 No right of withdrawal 3 Double taxation of profits
S-corporation (if available)	1 Same benefits of corporation flow-through of taxation	1 Complex, double filings
Limited liability company	1 Not subject to restrictions on finance. 2 No rules concerning discrimination within classes of ownership interests. 3 Right of member to withdraw and receive fair market value. 4 Member's contribution to LLC can be made in form of obligation to perform future services. 5 Tax advantages flow through with income and losses. 6 Can get in and out of LLC tax free; a Corporation has to liquidate.	1 Some uncertainty since LLC is fairly new.

- *Number of owners in business.* If there are many owners of a business, you really need to think about forming a business entity since the ownership would be difficult to manage otherwise. If there are multiple owners, have documents prepared regulating the contributions of the owners, their rights and responsibilities and mechanisms to transfer interests and the business. Without a carefully drawn agreement among the owners, such items as owners' withdrawal, death and disability can literally cripple a business. Carefully spell out everyone's obligations and provide a carefully worded transfer provision.

- *Nature of the business.* Naturally, the type of business has some impact on its form. Any business that is inherently risky should be in the corporation or limited liability company form.

- *Marketing considerations.* From a marketing standpoint, you might use your form of business entity to position yourself. For example, a consulting practice in the limited liability company format might appear more impressive than a sole proprietorship. All other things being equal, Marketing Research Consultants, LLC might have a more professional ring to it than John Doe and Associates. Consequently, depending upon how you wish to position your business in the marketplace, you might choose a legal entity. In that case, the cost of the additional expense might be worth it from a marketing standpoint. In addition, the formation of a business entity allows you to protect the name to a certain degree and use that name for your business.

- *Duration of the enterprise.* Generally, the longer that you intend to have the business, the more important that you have an entity that can carry on the business. If you intend to try to transfer your business down to other generations, you might then want to use a form of business entity.

- *Projected profits and losses.* This is related to tax consequences. If you are projecting some losses at the inception of your business, you might wish to adapt a flow-through structure so that you can use any losses from your business to offset other income.

Chateau Orleans
Bed & Breakfast

Kathryn and Jean Paul visit both an accountant and an attorney before making the decision regarding their choice of legal entity. Since their primary asset will be a bed & breakfast, which is real property, they are counselled to choose a flow-through entity for purposes of taxation. They are also concerned about liability. Even though their inn will constitute the bulk of their personal assets, they see no reason to be liable personally for any claim against their facility. Consequently, they decide on a limited liability company, which meets their objectives perfectly. It provides the flow-through taxation as well as the limited liability. Although there are some costs to maintain, these costs are inconsequential when considering the benefits that they will provide the owners. Even though they are married, Kathryn and Jean Paul set forth all of the pertinent rights and understandings regarding their venture in the operating agreement.

Summary

1   The proper choice of your form of business or business entity is very important for the small business, so give this careful consideration.

2   The main factors to consider in choosing your form of legal entity are tax implications, owner's liability, ease of use, opportunity to grow with the business and cost to maintain.

3   Depending upon the jurisdiction that your business is in, the types of legal entities available include the sole proprietorship, the partnership, the limited partnership, the corporation and the limited liability company.

Action step

■   Consult your attorney and accountant, weigh the various factors and then choose your form of business organization.

CHAPTER NINE

Advanced business law – avoiding the courthouse, intellectual property and other important legal issues

> Agree with thine adversary quickly, while thou art in the way
> with him; lest at any time the adversary delivers thee to the
> judge, and the judge delivers thee to the officer, and thee be
> cast into prison.
>
> (Holy Bible – Matthew 5:25–26)

The fundamentals of avoiding disputes

Throughout this book, I have recommended the use of attorneys in the appropriate circumstances. However, one use of attorneys that you want to avoid is with respect to litigation or legal claims involving your business. It is better to take definite steps in your business practices to avoid controversies. With very few exceptions, controversies that lead to litigation are a serious waste of time and resources of your business.

As the above quotation from the Bible illustrates, it is generally advisable 'to agree with thine adversary quickly.' If you don't get along with others, it is possible that 'the judge' could ultimately deliver 'thee to the officer' who could cast you into prison. While this is good religious advice, it is also good legal advice. Make the effort to get along with your neighbour. If you rely on the courts, you might end up with a very unfavourable result. Courts can be extremely unpredictable. Consequently, it makes much more sense to either avoid or quickly resolve your disputes and then get back to business.

During my career practising law, I have seen many issues end up in court unnecessarily. The resulting litigation was generally disruptive to the business, in addition to being expensive. Much of it could have been avoided with a meeting to correct the misunderstanding. In some cases, a simple apology would have been all that was necessary. Instead, the parties wasted their time and resources. Therefore, it is a prudent practice to do business in a manner that avoids misunderstandings, controversies and lawsuits. This requires that you

1   do business in a courteous and ethical manner;

2   avoid misunderstandings by reducing your understandings and agreements to writing;

3   avoid doing business with people who do not operate in a similar manner.

Operate in a courteous, ethical manner.

In our fast-paced, technology-driven society, there is sometimes a tendency to neglect common courtesy in our dealings with others. But people are still people and have the same feelings and emotions. Do business in a manner that respects the emotions of others. A little common courtesy goes a long way in building goodwill and avoiding controversy. More litigation than you can imagine starts when people are rubbed up the wrong way. It is often hurt feelings, as opposed to genuine legal controversies, that make their way into courtrooms.

Therefore, be sure that you and any of your employees treat others, including your customers, clients, suppliers, competitors and vendors, with respect and courtesy. Remember that sometimes it is better to get along than to be right. If you make a mistake, admit it readily rather than try to justify your actions.

Another way to avoid litigation and controversy is to conduct your business in an ethical, straightforward manner. Mean what you say and say what you mean. Make it a practice to honour all of your commitments. Do what you say that you're going to do. A good corollary to this is – don't make promises you can't keep. There's nothing that irritates others more than broken commitments. Make your word your bond. Not only will others respect you more, but you will find that you also avoid controversy.

Avoid misunderstandings – put agreements in writing

Another way to avoid misunderstandings that could lead to controversy is to put your agreements in writing. This does not necessarily have to be formal writing, just something that is clear and sets forth the main points of the understanding. Note that whenever you set forth the main points of the understanding with which the other party agrees, you've just created a contract.

I would generally recommend an attorney for complicated contracts, such as the sale of a business or a major commercial contract. However, simple understandings, such as the terms of a particular order, do not require legal assistance. Be clear in setting forth the terms of the understanding. For example, my printer requires that I initial all final copies of brochures or flyers before they are actually printed. While this might seem like a very simple practice, it does confirm in writing that I am in agreement with the accuracy and form of the printed piece before hundreds or perhaps thousands are printed. This sets forth a clear understanding between us about what is going to be printed. This is one type of written understanding that avoids disputes. There are many others. Make it a business practice to confirm things in writing as much as possible. You could put all of the essential terms of your products or services on an invoice. Or you could send a letter or prepare a formal proposal.

Be aware though that you can enter into a binding contract without the necessity of writing. So be careful with your verbal promises, so that they do not contradict your written understanding. Any time you give a verbal representation which is later accepted, you have created a contract. It is better to do business in writing because verbal contracts can be difficult to enforce.

Much of the world of contracts is based upon English common law. Even areas that have adopted their own commercial or civil code with respect to contractual understandings are based on English common law. Under English common law, the components of a contract include

- the offer;

- the acceptance;

- consideration.

Although most contracts do not have to be in writing, the Statute of Frauds requires some contracts, such as the sale of real estate, to be in writing. The specific elements of a contract are as follows:

1   *Offer.* A proposal or an offer that is unequivocal and states all the important parts of an understanding is considered an offer. Once an offer is made, a contract can be formed by simple acceptance. As a result, exercise care when you make an offer because it might just be accepted and you would be contractually bound. For example, a Seller offers to sell a Buyer 10 widgets at 10 dollars apiece.

2   *Acceptance.* An assent or response to the offer that complies in all material respects to the offer itself is known as acceptance of the offer and creates a contract. If the Seller in the above example says 'I accept', then there is an acceptance and a contract has been created. But the acceptance or assent to the contract has to comply in material respects to the offer itself. In the above example, if the Buyer agreed to buy five widgets at 10 dollars apiece, then this would not be a valid acceptance since the offer was for *10* widgets. The Seller's response is actually a counter offer, which starts the offer and acceptance process all over again.

3   *Counter offer.* As was indicated in the above example, a counter offer is created when the response to an offer differs materially from the offer itself. The counter offer actually becomes a new offer, which can itself then be accepted by the original Seller by agreement with its terms. In the example above, the Seller *could* accept the Buyer's counter offer and agree to sell five widgets at 10 dollars apiece, thus creating a contract. But the Seller would not have to.

4   *Consideration.* In addition to the offer and acceptance, the contract also needs to contain consideration in order to be binding. Although the concept of consideration can be a little difficult to understand, the point is that both parties must need to commit something in order for there to be a binding contract. In a simple purchase of goods, the consideration by the Buyer is the financial commitment of the purchase. The Seller's consideration is the promise to sell you the particular goods at a particular price. In a commercial setting, most contracts have ample consideration. However, when one side fails to make a promise, there might be a lack of consideration. As a general rule of thumb, agreements that are one sided in the area of commitment probably lack adequate consideration and might therefore be unenforceable.

5   *Essential terms.* As stated previously, in order for a contract to be binding there must be agreement over the essential contract terms. In a commercial setting, these two major terms include the *price* and

the *quantity*. Other types of agreements might have different essential terms, which would depend upon the nature of the business. The point is, if the essential terms are agreed to in the contracts, a binding contract would be formed.

6   *Statute of Frauds*. Contracts which are formed orally can present a problem in proof. In most jurisdictions, contracts concerning the sale of real estate and other types of contracts have to be in writing. As a practical matter, it's best to put all major understandings in writing to avoid any misunderstanding.

MORAL: Get into the habit of putting major understandings in writing. This not only protects you legally, but fortifies your legal position should it be challenged.

Avoid problem people

A final way to avoid unnecessary litigation is to avoid problem people. In my experience, there are some people who are continually involved in controversy. They are either being sued or are threatening to sue others. Their business practices are either unethical or sloppy or both. You know the type. Just avoid them.

Arbitration and mediation

One of the more positive developments with respect to the legal system is the growing use of alternative dispute resolution as a means of resolving disputes before going to court. The two major forms of alternative dispute resolution are arbitration and mediation.

Arbitration provides a substitute for the traditional civil litigation process of resolving disputes. The point of arbitration is to forgo the sometimes cumbersome and time consuming process of civil litigation and put all of the power and authority of the court system into a single arbitrator, whose decision is final. Arbitration can end up streamlining the resolution process because the civil litigation process, particularly in the United States, has become very unwieldy. The arbitration process is generally much quicker and more efficient than civil litigation.

Commercial contracts can specify that any dispute therein will be settled by arbitration. However, you must be careful that you have an independent arbitrator, since in many cases the arbitration is binding.

Many international contracts select a well-known arbitrator such as the Hague in the Netherlands, to avoid potential local bias.

Unlike arbitration, mediation is not binding. The parties are free to walk away from mediation at any time. The point of mediation is to inject the viewpoint of an independent third party into the dispute. It is then the goal of the mediator to see if common ground can be reached. Often the parties become very grounded in their position and the input of the mediator can help break the impasse. Although most commercial contracts do not contain mediation clauses similar to arbitration clauses, the parties can agree to try to mediate the dispute, before turning to the legal process.

Protect your intellectual property

In today's communications and technology-driven business world, the intellectual property or technology of a business is becoming increasingly important. Intellectual property can be thought of as the intangible parts of the business such as technology, innovations, or unique processes, procedures or designs. Many businesses have intellectual property and don't even know it. Intellectual property protection does not apply only to software developers and inventors; it is relevant to any business with an idea, presentation, concept, logo, slogan, tradename or a unique way of operating. All of this can be subject to proprietary protections. Your intellectual property can be a significant value for your business. Therefore, recognize it and protect it.

Although the discussion of world-wide intellectual property protection is beyond the scope of this book, I will present an overview so that at least you can be aware of some intellectual property issues. In the United States and other parts of the world, there are three levels of protection for intellectual property:

- patent;
- trademark;
- copyright.

Patent

Patent protection is considered the highest level of protection for an idea. You would generally obtain a patent in those countries in which you do business. If you are not already tired of me recommending attorneys, let me say that you really need a patent or intellectual property attorney to assist you in obtaining a patent. Patents are a very intricate and specialized area of the law. The patent process is also arduous, time consuming and expensive. Therefore it would require a very good idea with commercial potential to be worth the trouble and expense of a patent. Many entrepreneurs contact me all excited about some particular discovery or application. However, generally very little of what I see merits patent protection.

But don't let me deter you, if you really think that your idea or invention is unique enough. The first step in the process involves a patent search to determine if there are similar ideas or patents on the market. Often a patent search can be done by a service whose rates are generally much cheaper than those of a patent attorney. In fact, before you spend too much time on an invention, you might want to determine if the technology has already been patented. A business consultant told me the story of an inventor who spent seven years in his basement working on a particular electronic application. When the inventor finally invited an outside team to evaluate his technology, he received some bad news. The electronic application he was working on was already in existence and had been for a number of years. So start first with a patent search. If the search is favourable, your next step is to consult a patent attorney. A good patent attorney will inform you whether or not your idea is worth patent protection and how much it would cost.

Trademark

A trademark is a more common form of intellectual property for the small business. It can be any work, name, symbol or device or any combination thereof adopted and used by a person to identify goods made and sold by them from goods made and sold by others. Generally, only distinctive trademarks may be registered. The marks that are unique and do not describe the product or service are given the most protection. Examples of trademarks include the Coca-Cola logo or the McDonald's arches.

It is much more likely that your business will have the occasion to protect a trademark than to obtain a patent. Usually the registration of a trademark at the national level, in the area in which you do business, provides the strongest protection. However, there is some expense involved and you must determine whether or not such protection is worth the expense. In some jurisdictions, you can obtain common-law trademark protection by using the goods in interstate commerce and noting that you have a trademark. Although this protection is not as good as a registered trademark, it is certainly better than nothing. However, you cannot say that you have a registered trademark, sometimes noted as the symbol ®, if you haven't completed the registration. In addition to registering your trademark on a national level, it is also possible to register it on a local level. If you are doing business only in that locality, then this registration might provide you with an acceptable level of protection. Your decision to trademark on a national level should be made in connection with the likelihood that you will expand. Like any decision involving intellectual property, you must balance the benefits and costs of protection.

Tradename

Your tradename is the name under which you do business. It is very important that the business protects its tradename, since that is how it represents itself to the consuming public. Failure to protect your tradename from competitors can result in significant confusion and loss of business. One advantage of forming a legal entity is that it can provide you with a legally protected tradename.

Copyright

Copyright attaches to a work as soon as it is fixed in some tangible form. Generally, the original author of the work is the owner of the copyright. Copyright protection extends to original works of authorship fixed in any tangible medium of expression.

Note though, that copyright protection does not extend to any idea, procedure, process, concept or principle. The notice of copyright includes: the symbol © or the word Copyright, the year of first publication and name of owner. Generally, the term of the copyright extends throughout the author's life plus 50 years after the author's death.

Note that with the advent of the Internet, there is much copyright material that is available for downloading. The Internet has made it very easy to violate copyright material by the ease with which something can be downloaded or integrated into other material. Always copyright any information that you send out or that you post on the Internet. Use the symbol ©, to indicate the common-law copyright, which arises the moment that you create the work. Take the small step to note an interest in your original work, and you can take a large step towards protecting that interest.

Don't infringe on intellectual property

An important corollary to protecting your own intellectual property is to not infringe on the intellectual property of others. In addition to legal sanctions, infringement can result in civil and criminal penalties, depending upon your jurisdiction. Also, it is a bad business practice that can prove very embarrassing. Strategies to avoid infringing the intellectual property of others include the following:

- *Avoidance.* Be aware of what trademarks or service marks currently are the protected intellectual property of others and simply avoid using or infringing on the copyright.

- *Release.* Sometimes the owners of the copyright will release the copyright to you in order that you can use it. Sometimes this release has to be bargained for and other times the owner will release it to you to get some publicity.

- *Contractual indemnity.* If part of your business involves using a logo for public relations, it is possible to obtain the indemnification of the person who is allowing you to use the trademark.

Negotiation strategies

Earlier in the chapter, I recommended adopting certain policies and practices to avoid controversy. This is not to say that you have to necessarily disadvantage yourself in your dealings with others. Quite the contrary; you are in business to make a profit and your activities should be directed to that end. It will be helpful to examine some negotiating skills that could assist you in your business. At many points during an entrepreneur's business, the entrepreneur needs to negotiate. Most business owners are negotiating every day, with suppliers, with customers and with people in the same business.

By negotiation strategy, I don't mean a strategy to take advantage of someone else. The stereotype of the hardened negotiator squeezing their adversary into submission is just a stereotype. Actually, it is those who can work with the people they are negotiating with who end up with the best bargains in their business. The point is to look for the proverbial win/win in your dealings. If you think this way, then people will be lining up to do business with you.

Remember that you're not trying to win at someone else's expense. Rather, you want to reach an outcome that benefits both parties. Entrepreneurs who are obsessed with obtaining the upper hand in every dealing quickly find themselves without customers to sell to or vendors to buy from.

Consider the other's position

Most people enter a negotiation focused on one thing – their position. However, this is not always the best strategy. By ignoring the other party, you miss the opportunity for any compromise that would be beneficial to everyone.

Start by separating the people from the negotiation. Do not become overly focused on a particular person, or you will lose your objectivity. Next, focus on the other party's interest and not just your position. By focusing on others you can keep in mind ways to satisfy the party often at no detriment to yourself. Pay attention to what the other party really wants. You may just be able to fulfil it with little cost to yourself.

For example, suppose a customer unexpectedly insists that your product be delivered to them personally, even though your original understanding required the customer to pick up the goods. Resist the impulse to focus on your position only and look for a way to help the other party. Even though you might be on firm legal ground, consider a way to satisfy the customer. Where does the customer need the goods to be ultimately delivered? Suppose the customer plans to take that product to a third location? Could you send it via two-day mail to that location? Would that be acceptable to the customer who would also agree to pay the shipping? The point of this simple example is to focus on solutions, rather than your position, even though the customer was supposed to pick up the product in the first place.

Stages of negotiation

The different stages of the negotiating process include analysis, planning and discussion. Before entering any negotiation process, whether selling your product or preparing a proposal, be sure to do your homework. Take the time to analyse what you think the other party's needs are in this case. Then plan out your situation with them. Work out the arguments and the tactics that you will take during the negotiation process.

The next phase is discussion. Keep the discussion objective and do not resort to personalities. Focus on mutual gain rather than on being right. Remember that negotiators are people first.

During the negotiation process, don't hesitate to take a 'timeout' if something does not feel right. Tell the party that you will get back to them and request additional time. I've found in my own experience that whenever I was rushed or pressured into a decision, it was invariably the wrong one. In fact, pressuring someone into a decision is a negotiating technique used by the other side, usually to get people to do something that they would not do otherwise. Be very wary if someone tries to pressure you and will not give you any additional time.

One of the best solutions to avoid being pressured into a hasty decision is to develop alternatives. Developing alternatives is part of the planning phase. It is never wise to go into a situation that involves bargaining without alternatives. If you know under what terms the other suppliers will sell you similar goods, then you have an option when you negotiate with a particular supplier. Therefore it is much less likely that you'll be pressured.

Beware negotiating tricks

The unsuspecting person can often fall subject to some traditional negotiating tricks. The key is to recognize these tricks and let the other party know that you are aware of them. These tricks include:

- *Good guy, bad guy.* This involves a tag team negotiation process where one of the parties tries to be reasonable while the other one tries to be aggressive. This is often used by police officers in questioning suspects and is designed to wear the other party down.

- *False deadlines.* This is very similar to trying to pressure someone to make a decision and can be simply responded to by refusing to yield to the pressure. 'I understand that you're as anxious to conclude this matter as am I, but I need to check something and get back to you'.

- *Personal attacks.* The other party hopes to distract you from your position by having you respond to a personal attack.

- *Lack of decision-making authority.* This technique is often employed in automobile dealerships when the salesperson denies that they can agree to anything without going to their 'manager.' With this, they hope to gain as much flexibility as possible without committing themselves. In this case, you want to insist upon negotiating with a person with a proper decision-making authority.

A good summary of the negotiation process is as follows:

- Do your homework. Never enter a serious negotiation without a list of the other possible alternatives. Know before going into the negotiation where you could buy or sell a similar product or service elsewhere.

- Always keep a good relationship with the other party despite the fact that the negotiations might get heated. This requires you to separate people out from the problem. Never resort to a personal attack that questions someone's intelligence or motives, but keep coolly focused on the problem.

- Prepare a list of the possible interests of the other party. If the negotiation is involved enough, it helps to have a full understanding of the other party's interest.

- Always look for several options that can satisfy someone's interest. While they might be insisting on something in particular, they may very well be satisfied with another option that you can easily deliver. However unless this point is raised, the other party will not be focused at all or be thinking about this option.

Summary

1   Avoid controversies in your business by dealing with people in a courteous, straightforward and ethical manner.

2   Avoid misunderstandings by putting your contracts and agreements in writing to the greatest extent possible. The writing does not have to be involved, only clear with respect to the major terms.

3   Under the common law of contracts and commercial codes, binding contracts can be created with a valid offer and acceptance of the essential contract terms.

4   Protect your own intellectual property and avoid infringing on the intellectual property of others.

5   Develop a rational negotiation process in your business dealings, which involves doing your homework and focusing on the interests of the other party.

CHAPTER TEN

Introduction to accounting – accounting can be fun

All things are difficult before they are easy.

(John Norley)

Accounting can be fun

Well, maybe not exactly fun. But if accounting is approached properly, it can at least be tolerable. I have taught accounting at college level and in my entrepreneurship courses and know first hand the difficulties that some have with accounting. Those not inclined to accounting can find its principles mind numbing and confusing. Actually, I can sympathize because I initially had trouble with accounting when I was in graduate business school. In fact, I nearly failed my first accounting test, even though I had frantically prepared for it. Eventually I realized that I was not approaching accounting properly. The first mistake I made was to allow myself to become intimidated by the subject. After all, with its big bulky text, wasn't accounting supposed to be difficult? My second mistake was to try to *memorize* the accounting principles. Memorization was the way that I had approached other academic subjects, usually with success. I couldn't figure out why it wasn't working with accounting.

Finally, I realized that the key to *learning* accounting was to first really *understand the basics*. Once I understood the basics, I could then branch out and learn some of the more complicated twists and turns of accounting. My initial approach was to try to learn everything at once, which was both overwhelming and frustrating.

Accounting is important to the business owner for several reasons. To begin with, accounting is often called the language of business. Its essential terms and principles are used and relied upon throughout the financial world, including bankers and investors. Accounting can also be described as a method of measuring, describing and interpreting economic activity. In other words, it lets you know how your business is doing. In addition, accounting can provide the financial information that you can use for managing your business.

Despite the volumes of material on accounting, there are really just a few accounting principles that you need to master as a business owner. Your goal is to become 'financially literate', so that you can understand the 'financial vital signs' of your business. Although I still recommend the use of accounting professionals, the business owner needs to understand the financial vital signs of their business and monitor them on a regular basis. In order to do this, the owner needs to understand some fundamental accounting principles.

All financial management starts with understanding your 'financial vital signs', the understanding of which is based on two accounting principles:

1   the dynamic principle of the cash flow statement;

2   the static principle of the balance sheet.

FIGURE 10.1   Keys to understanding your financial vital signs

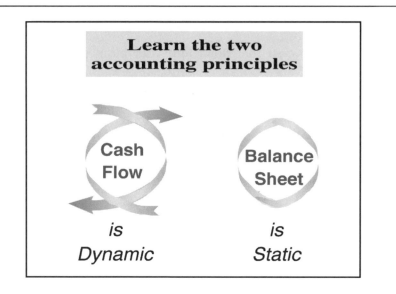

Dynamic principle – cash flow statement

Think of the cash flow statement as the 'dynamic' principle of accounting, which measures the change in or performance of a business over a period of time. You are probably familiar with the term *income statement* as a measure of business performance. However, for our purposes, we will focus on the *cash flow statement*. The major difference between the income statement and the cash flow statement involves the use of *accrual* accounting principles, which affect the *timing* of revenue and expense recognition. Under accrual accounting, revenues and expenses are recognized when they are *incurred* and not necessarily when the *cash* changes hands. For example, under accrual accounting, revenue would be recognized when you send out an invoice. You would accrue the income for income statement purposes and it would become an account receivable. In addition, expenses would be recognized when you receive a bill and would become an account payable.

Although most businesses operate on an accrual basis for tax purposes, some still use a cash basis. Rather than worry about accrual accounting right now, let's focus exclusively on the cash flow statement. Not only does this simplify matters, but it puts the financial focus where it belongs – *cash*. With cash flow problems the leading cause of mortality for the small business, the cash flow statement is the single most important financial vital sign for the entrepreneur.

Simply put, the cash flow statement details:

1 *cash in*: the cash that flows into your business in the form of revenues;

2 *cash out*: the cash that then flows out of your business in the form of expenses.

Cash in – revenues

Cash flows into your business in two forms. One way is in the form of capital contributions and loan proceeds. However, for purposes of the cash flow statement we are focusing on financial performance. Consequently, we are focusing on the money that flows into your business in the form of revenues. Revenues are the source of cash for your business and would include the money that you receive for the sales of your goods and services. If you sell goods on account, then for purposes of your cash

FIGURE 10.2 Cash flow statement

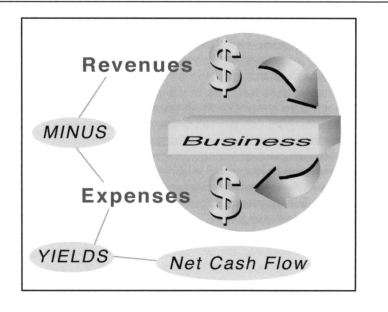

flow statement, those sales are not recognized as revenues until the cash flows into your business.

Revenues

Cash in – revenues   Amount of money that flows into a business through the sale of its goods and services. Does not include money that flows into the business in the form of loans and capital contributions

Cash out – expenses

Expenses are the uses of cash in your business. Simply put, expenses are the cash payments out of your business for the various bills and charges of your business. These expenses are subtracted from your revenues to determine cash flow. Calculating the cash flow statement is very similar to calculating your bank balance and reconciling your bank account. Think of the deposits to your account as your revenues and the cheques that you write as your expenses. At the end of the banking cycle, you have your ending balance. The cash flow statement involves the exact same process. Cash in. Cash out. In addition, just as you write cheques for your different bills, the cash flow statement also assigns expenses into categories. These categories are referred to as your *chart of accounts*, which serves to break down the various expenses by category.

Figure 10.3 is an example of a chart of accounts.

FIGURE 10.3   Chart of accounts

Item	Description
Advertising	Advertising and marketing costs
Inventory	Your inventory costs
Insurance	Cost to insure your property
Licences	Occupational licences
Loan payments	Repayment of any debt
Maintenance	Repairs and maintenance expenses
Miscellaneous expenses	Miscellaneous items
Payroll	Salaries and wages
Professional fees	Legal, accounting and other fees
Rent	Payments to your landlord
Supplies	Supplies for your business
Taxes	Sales, income and payroll
Telephone	Telephone and fax services
Utilities	Electricity, water and gas

This chart of accounts should provide a general idea of the various categories of cash expenses for your business. Naturally each business will be different. In some cases the expenses for one of the categories listed in Figure 10.3 will be very significant and you might want to break that expense out into various sub-categories. However, calculating the expense portion of your cash flow statement is nothing more than assigning the various expenses to the chart of accounts.

The two steps of calculating revenues in and determining expenses out comprise the cash flow statement. As we will see in the next chapter, one of the most important uses of the cash flow statement by the entrepreneur is to prepare pro forma cash flow statements for future operations. Naturally, preparing pro forma statements is considerably easier if you have previous cash flow statements to draw from. Preparing pro forma cash flow statements for the brand new startup can be a bit tricky. This involves not only correctly categorizing and calculating your revenues and expenses, but also estimating them. As we will see, the most important thing about this process is to analyse and prepare the assumptions behind your estimates. Often estimating your revenues and expenses are as much of an art as a science. The best policy is to use a range of estimates so that you can calculate a worst-case and a best-case scenario. Many businesses have been sunk because the owners have been too optimistic in estimating cash flows and operating profits of the business.

One important suggestion in establishing your chart of accounts is to carefully estimate each one of your accounts. Resist the temptation to straight line the accounts, which is to use the same figure all the way across your monthly estimations. Think carefully about fluctuations in your business and whether some accounts might fluctuate slightly. We will discuss preparing pro forma cash flow statements in the next chapter.

Static principle – balance sheet

The next accounting principle involves the *balance sheet*, which can be thought of as the static principle of accounting. Rather than measure the ongoing flow of economic activity, the balance sheet is a snapshot in time. In fact, just about every accounting text that I've ever seen always describes the balance sheet as a 'snapshot in time'. However, subsequent explanations tend to become very complicated, very fast. I will try to keep things simple for you.

In preparing your balance sheet, the first item to consider is the *assets* of your business. Assets are those identifiable items that contribute to the operation of the business and can therefore be thought of as resources. Assets include such items as your cash, furniture, inventory, and supplies. The next item on the balance sheet is your *liabilities*. Your liabilities are all of the debts of the business such as trade accounts and notes payable. Since your liabilities represent claims on your assets, they are subtracted from your assets to determine your *owner's equity*, which is the final item of the balance sheet. Think of the owner's equity as the plug-in figure between your assets and liabilities. It is not necessarily the cash of your business, but rather the amount left over after all of the claims of your creditors have been accounted for. From an accounting sense, the owner's equity represents all of the capital that you have contributed to the business plus its net profits.

As the above figure indicates, there are two ways to view the balance sheet principles. One way is with the following equation:

Assets – liabilities = owner's equity.

In that case, you would identify your assets, then subtract your liabilities. The amount left after subtracting your liabilities is your net or owner's equity. Another way to consider the balance sheet is to shift liabilities to the other side of the equation:

Assets = liabilities + owner's equity.

This is another way of viewing the balance sheet. In this case, your assets are equal to your liabilities plus your owner's equity. In other words, the assets of your business can be thought of as having two sets of claims on

FIGURE 10.4 Balance sheet principles

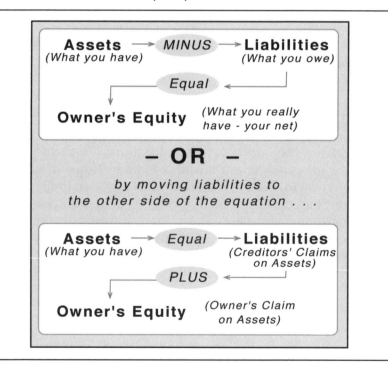

them. One claim is based upon the liabilities owed to your creditors. The next claim would be the owner's and would entitle the owner to anything that is not owed to your creditors.

That is the fundamental way of setting up the balance sheet. Assets and liabilities are then placed into categories and the difference between the two, or the 'plug figure', is the owner's equity. This provides a fairly logical and well-understood way of providing that snapshot in time of the business. More importantly, the balance sheet provides a springboard for ratio analysis and to determine the financial solvency of your business. A balance sheet is depicted in Figure 10.5.

The balance sheet is very similar to a personal financial statement. If you have ever completed a financial statement in connection with a loan, you have had to list all of your assets and your liabilities. On one side of the financial statement, you listed your cash, stocks, bonds and any real estate. On the other side of the financial statement you listed any credit card, notes or mortgage liability. The difference is your net worth. The balance sheet is identical to the personal financial statement, only the net worth is referred to as your owner's equity.

The interrelationship between the cash flow statement and the balance sheet is shown in Figure 10.6. As is illustrated, the net cash flow of your business flows into owner's equity. This net cash flow then becomes part of the retained earnings of the business.

Understanding the dynamic accounting principle of the cash flow statement and the static accounting principle of the balance sheet are the primary two prerequisites to your becoming financially literate as a business owner. Mastering these principles not only equips you to monitor your financial vital signs, but also enables you to perform more involved financial management analysis for your business. This analysis involves ratios and comparisons to your financial statements.

Connie's Coffee Shop

We will illustrate the balance sheet and the cash flow statement with the example of Connie's Coffee Shop. Connie is a retired schoolteacher who has always wanted to open a coffee shop. So she buys $3,000 of coffee

FIGURE 10.5   Balance sheet

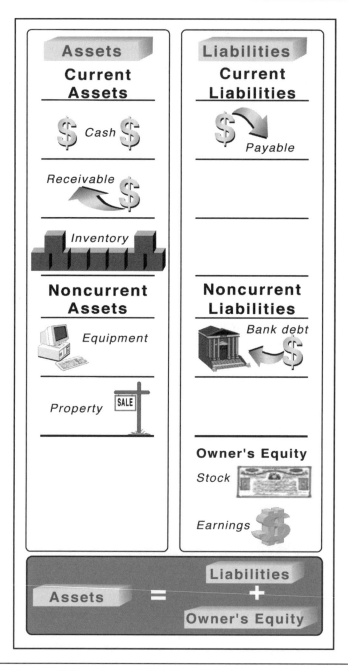

Note: See Chapter 12 for a more detailed discussion of current and non current assets and liabilities.

FIGURE 10.6 Relationship between the cash flow statement and the balance sheet

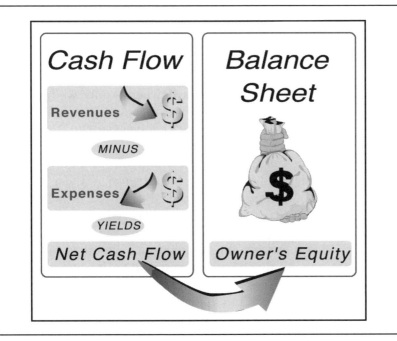

equipment, $1,000 of computer equipment, $1,000 of coffee from a wholesaler on credit, contributes $10,000 of her savings, and borrows $10,000 from her father. She obtains the proper licences, opens up a bank account, signs the lease, cleans up the building and on the first of the month opens Connie's Coffee Shop. Can we set up a balance sheet for these activities – yes!

Let's start first by calculating the assets of Connie's Coffee Shop:

$10,000 – cash from savings

$ 3,000 – coffee equipment

$ 1,000 – computer equipment

$ 1,000 – inventory (coffee)

$10,000 – loan proceeds from father (even though a loan still does represent $10,000 in cash for the business)

$25,000 in total assets

Next, let's calculate the liabilities:

$10,000 – loan from her father

$ 1,000 – account payable to coffee wholesaler

_____

$11,000 in total liabilities

Under our equation, assets − liabilities = owner's equity, we would have $25,000 − $11,000 = $14,000. Another way to look at this would be assets ($25,000) = liabilities ($11,000) + owner's equity ($14,000). Now let's set up a balance sheet (see Figure 10.7).

Note how you calculate the assets and the liabilities, with the owner's equity being the difference between the two, or the 'plug figure'. But the owner's equity can be independently derived. Remember that Connie contributed $10,000 of cash and $4,000 of equipment. That totals the $14,000 of owner's equity, which was contributed to the business. The inventory of $1,000 was bought on credit and the other $10,000 was generated by a loan. Although both the cash and the inventory are assets,

FIGURE 10.7   Connie's Coffee Shop – balance sheet

CONNIE'S COFFEE SHOP
BALANCE SHEET

Assets	=	Liabilities +	Owner's equity
Cash	$20,000	Loan Payable $10,000	Original Investment $14,000
Equipment	3,000	Account Payable $ 1,000	
Computer	1,000		
Inventory	1,000		
Total	**$25,000**		**Total $25,000**

Or the equation can be changed to the following:

Assets	=	Liabilities +	
Cash	$20,000	Loan Payable $10,000	
Equipment	3,000	Account Payable $ 1,000	
Computer	1,000		
Inventory	1,000	**Owner's Equity** $14,000	
Total	**$25,000**	**Total $25,000**	

they in fact entered the business with the accompanying liabilities and are therefore netted out.

Summary

1   It is important for every business owner to become 'financially literate' to be able to understand the 'financial vital signs' of their business.

FIGURE 10.8   Connie's coffee shop – revenues and expenses

The first year of operations for Connie's Coffee Shop produced revenues or cash into the business of $58,500.

1st Year

REVENUES	$58,500

In addition, there were total expenses of $45,600

CHART OF ACCOUNTS

Item	Amount
Advertising	$1,500
Inventory	$11,000
Insurance	$1,000
Licences	$450
Loan payments	$2,000
Maintenance	$750
Miscellaneous expenses	$350
Payroll	$14,000
Professional Fees	$1,250
Rent	$6,000
Supplies	$1,600
Telephone	$2,100
Utilities	$3,600
Total	**$45,600**

FIGURE 10.9   Connie's coffee shop – cash flow statement

CONNIE'S COFFEE SHOP
CASH FLOW STATEMENT

Revenues			$58,500
Expenses			
	Advertising	$1,500	
	Insurance	$1,000	
	Inventory	$11,000	
	Licences	$450	
	Loan payments	$2,000	
	Maintenance	$750	
	Miscellaneous	$350	
	Payroll	$14,000	
	Professional Fees	$1,250	
	Rent	$6,000	
	Supplies	$1,600	
	Telephone	$2,100	
	Utilities	$3,600	
Total Expenses			45,600
Cash Flow			$12,900

2   The two accounting principles behind the 'financial vital signs' of the business are the dynamic concept of the cash flow statement and the static concept of the balance sheet.

3   Small businesses should focus on the cash flow statement instead of the income statement, since cash is of paramount importance to the small business.

4   The balance sheet is a snapshot in time. It can be represented by the equation assets = liabilities + owner's equity.

5   The balance sheet and the cash flow statement are interrelated.

CHAPTER ELEVEN

Preparing startup expenses and pro forma financials

> One of life's most painful moments comes when we must admit that we didn't do our homework, that we are not prepared.
>
> (Merlin Olsen)

Now that we have established a basic understanding of the cash flow statement and the balance sheet, it is time to prepare some financial statements for your business. The financial statements can be thought of as the centrepiece of the business plan, the glue that holds the rest of the plan together. Remember that the business plan is an interrelated working document, with all of the sections dependent upon each other. Your financial section ties in the marketing and operations of your business and provides the hard data to predict and measure your results.

One of the first types of financial statements that any business owner has to prepare is one to determine their initial capital requirement. This statement is very similar to preparing your chart of accounts since you are estimating and categorizing your initial outlays. Naturally, you need to be as accurate as possible in determining your initial startup expenses so that they can be adequately financed. After estimating your startup expenses, the next step would be to prepare pro forma cash flow statements and balance sheets. Pro forma statements should initially be prepared for one year on a monthly basis, and then for two additional years on an annual basis. Pro forma projections not only give the owner a plan for their operations, but also provide them with the system to measure their results. Although predicting the future is never easy, this exercise can be very beneficial to the new business owner. Preparing the pro forma statements requires you to really analyse your projected operations. How much business can you do? What price can you obtain for your product or service? This would involve the preparing of a set of assumptions regarding your projected level of business from your marketing analysis. You would estimate your market share and on that, base your monthly revenues. Next, a projected chart of accounts would have to be prepared for your expenses. Once you have identified your expenses, try to estimate them on a monthly basis. Sometimes, a range of operations is desirable to be sure that you can survive in a worst-case scenario. Next you want to cumulate your monthly revenues and expenses into an annual statement. The final step would be to closely analyse your expenses or costs by separating out fixed and variable costs, which lets you determine your break-even point.

Determining your initial capital requirement

The first financial calculation of importance for the new business is to determine your initial capital requirement. Failing to properly estimate your startup capital can shut your business down before it even gets off the ground. Many budding entrepreneurs, in their zeal to get started, often overlook or underestimate items in determining their initial capital requirements. This can leave the business short of cash at its most critical time.

Table 11.1 illustrates the types of items that would be included in startup expenses.

Determining your initial capital needs requires that you set up a complete and accurate chart of accounts for startup expenses. This involves a certain amount of research and brainstorming. Table 11.1 is designed to present some general items to get you started. While the categories listed are general in nature, be aware that every business is different. Businesses have their own subtleties and their own needs. Find out all you can about your business so that you can be most accurate in determining these initial requirements.

One good tip in estimating your startup costs includes *research*. Yes, remember that from Chapter 5? Research your startup costs the same way that you researched your market. Call. Ask around. Get estimates. Many trade associations have this information and might be willing to share it with you as a prospective or future member. Don't assume anything. Take the time to confirm your projected cost as closely as possible. Find a similar business that is not a competitor and request information from the owner.

There is one item in the chart that deserves particular attention – working capital. Your working capital is those funds used to sustain

TABLE 11.1   Initial capital requirement

Startup expense	Explanation
1 Prepaid items, e.g. deposits	Don't forget any of your utility and rental deposits. Some leases require two months' deposit.
2 Inventory	If you make or sell products, you will need a startup inventory.
3 Professional fees	Use the techniques described in earlier chapters to negotiate the best fees for your attorney and your accountant.
4 Leasehold improvements	Remodelling or improvement expenses.
5 Industry specific costs	Depending on the industry, there are specific costs that are associated with the particular industry.
7 Office supplies and equipment	Even the smallest business can now obtain a fully equipped office. But do budget for your computer, your printer, stationery, cards and basic office supplies.
8 Marketing	Don't forget to budget for initial marketing costs. Direct marketing, print advertising, etc., are necessary to let your target market know about your new business.
9 Licences	The costs of some occupational licences are significant.
10 Taxes	Be sure that you budget sales taxes, payroll taxes, occupational taxes and other taxes that affect your business.
11 Working capital	Don't forget the working capital. Every business needs working capital until cash flow is sufficient to sustain operations.
12 Hidden costs	All businesses have hidden costs; the point is to figure them out and to budget for them.

operations during your startup phase before you become profitable. All new businesses need sufficient working capital in the beginning phase, but few budget properly for it. A good rule of thumb is to carefully estimate your working capital needs and then DOUBLE IT! That's right, calculate those funds that you think you might need to sustain operations and then double them. This might seem unduly conservative, but for the brand new startup, things never quite go just as planned. Give yourself plenty of time to reach a profitable stage.

After you've prepared an initial working capital requirement, compare it with your pro forma cash flow statement. You might want to then revise your working capital requirement. Then review your pro forma statement and set a range of scenarios based upon the likelihood of success of your business. Be sure that you have the money to sustain your worst-case scenario.

We will discuss financing your business later in this book. However, before you plan to finance the business, you have to determine how much money you think you will need. Although your initial capital requirement may appear daunting, it is much better to know your true capital needs up front. That is far superior to underestimating your capital and running out of money. This could happen even after you have sunk your life savings and have extended yourself and even your family for your business. Therefore, be accurate, even conservative, in determining your initial capital requirements.

Pro forma revenue

Estimating your market share

The first step in preparing your pro forma cash flow is to determine the amount of business that you will do during your first year. Refer back to the marketing analysis discussion of Chapter 5. In order to estimate your market share, you need to determine how big the market is and how much you think you can capture. Sometimes this can be expressed in a percentage of the market. Do you think you can get two to three per cent of this market? Consequently, you need to take your market share and then base your revenue figures below on the market share.

One way to estimate market share is to find out how similar businesses did during their first year. Remember the goal of this exercise is to be prepared – not be surprised.

FIGURE 11.1   Preparing pro forma financial statements

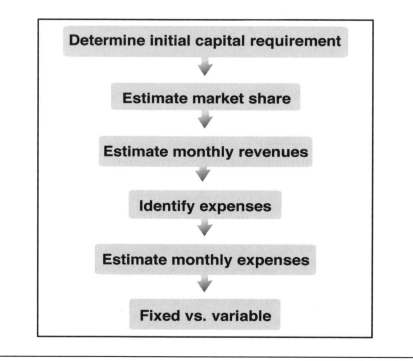

```
Determine initial capital requirement
                    ↓
        Estimate market share
                    ↓
      Estimate monthly revenues
                    ↓
           Identify expenses
                    ↓
      Estimate monthly expenses
                    ↓
          Fixed vs. variable
```

Estimating monthly revenues

Once you have determined your market share, the next step is to translate the market share into sales. If you can get two to three per cent of this market, how many customers and sales would that represent? Again your marketing research can help you estimate your revenue. Hopefully, you have determined that there is a sufficient market for your services and that you have a plan for capturing a defined amount of that market. Based upon what you have determined about the market, how many customers do you expect during a day? During a week? During a month? What price are you going to charge?

The more detailed your marketing research, the better idea you would have about this. Sometimes, good research can give you plenty of shortcuts in this area. For example, there might be data on how a similar business performed during its first year. Some trade associations can provide pro forma financials which detail revenues and expenses. People who are not in your specific market but a related one, might be willing to share information.

Estimating your revenue is also dependent upon your marketing plan. What types of marketing activities are you going to use to generate business? Are you going to use some type of penetration pricing strategy to crack the marketplace? If your marketing strategy involves penetration pricing, you need to determine the impact on your revenues. When in doubt, be conservative. Realize that it takes time to establish any business and that you might have to rely on your working capital for a while.

By determining your revenues on a monthly basis, you want to evaluate each month individually. Avoid the practice of 'straight lining' the accounts, which is to use the same revenue estimate for each month. Instead, consider all of the factors about your business. Is your business seasonal? In that case, you might reflect seasonal fluctuations on your revenue stream.

In addition, when you project your revenues in your business plan it is extremely helpful to footnote and even cross reference this part of the plan with your marketing information. For example, for Connie's Coffee Shop, Connie might have determined that the potential base for coffee spending in her geographic area is $400,000 per year. She estimates that she could obtain 10 per cent of this market or $40,000 per year during the first year.

I had a client who started a fast-food franchise in a similar industry that he had worked in for a number of years. Naturally, he knew a lot about the industry and even had very good industry information on similar establishments in the area. His pro forma financials were solidly based with research and experience. He knew the gross amount of the customer traffic, the amount spent by the average customer and what share of the market he could expect. Needless to say his loan was approved and it was no surprise that he reached his goals. He knew his market, his market share and numbers that they represented. He knew that there was sufficient market for his fast food establishment and the buying power of the area customers. With all of the relevant information about the customer profile and the market, plugging in the numbers proved very easy. I am pleased to say that his estimates turned out to be conservative and he is doing extremely well.

Pro forma expenses

Identifying and estimating monthly outlays

Preparing your pro forma expenses involves the same chart of accounts that was used in the previous chapter. Again, detail is very important here and it is important to estimate your expenses as much as possible. A good rule of thumb would be to use monthly and then annual estimations for your expenses. Your numbers are only as good as the assumptions and the research that you used to arrive at them. As we discussed earlier, resist the temptation to take a baseline figure and then 'straight line' the account across. The same seasonal fluctuations that affect your revenues also affect your expenses. Often, your costs will fluctuate in accordance with your revenues.

In preparing your pro forma expenses, you would use the chart of accounts from the previous chapter and estimate your costs on a monthly basis. Remember that detail is very important and your goal in estimating expenses is to avoid surprises.

Fixed vs. variable costs

One way to gain a better understanding of your expenses or costs is to divide them between fixed and variable costs. Once you have divided out fixed and variable costs, you can calculate break-even and have a better idea how your costs affect your net cash flow.

Fixed costs

Your fixed costs can be described as those costs that are fixed regardless of your level of business. They are costs that are essentially yours before you ever open your doors for your first customer. Fixed costs include your rent, utilities and other regular items that you have to pay, which are not dependent on your overhead. Another term for fixed costs is overhead. Types of fixed costs are:

- rent;
- utilities;

FIGURE 11.2   Fixed vs. variable costs

- note payments;

- professional fees;

- office supplies.

Variable costs

Unlike fixed costs, variable ones do vary directly with sales. They are costs that occur only if sales are made. Variable costs include those individual components needed to produce the goods, direct material and direct labour. Although variable costs are not as big an item in personal services, they are in manufacturing and retail. In all cases it is helpful to be able to distinguish between fixed and variable costs in establishing the prices for your goods. A good understanding of the relationship of your cost structure helps you to determine your all-important break-even point. Types of variable costs are:

- Direct materials: all of the costs involved in the goods that you sell form your direct materials cost. This would include the wholesale cost of materials, shipping costs and other costs of the product.

- Direct labour: the wages and salaries that are paid per unit of output. This would include any costs of labour to manufacture a product. In the case of Connie's Coffee Shop, the labour costs would include the people who staff the coffee shop.

Fixed and variable costs are general categories and arguments can be made that some labour is actually overhead and therefore a fixed cost. Some overhead can also be thought of as a variable cost. Those businesses in particularly cost-sensitive environments should go through this information carefully with their accountant. For our purposes, it suffices to understand enough of the basics of fixed and variable cost to prepare a break-even analysis.

Break-even analysis is illustrated in Figure 11.3. In order to perform break-even analysis you would take the following steps:

FIGURE 11.3   Break-even analysis

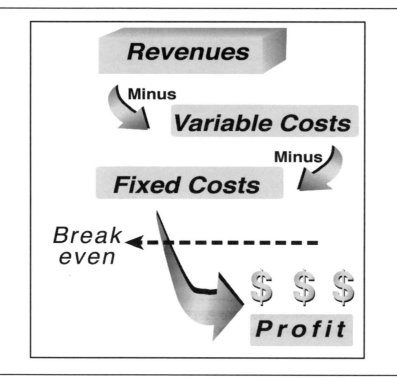

1   Separate your revenues, variable costs and fixed costs into separate categories. Remember that profit = revenues − variable costs − fixed costs.

2   Calculate the variable cost percentage, determined as follows:

Variable cost percentage: $\dfrac{\text{variable cost}}{\text{revenues}}$

3   Calculate the contribution margin. The contribution margin is the amount left after subtracting variable costs. The contribution margin is 100 per cent – variable cost percentage.

4   Calculate break-even revenues:

Break-even revenues: $\dfrac{\text{total fixed costs}}{\text{contribution margin}}$

Connie's Coffee Shop

Let's see whether or not we can determine the break-even point for Connie's Coffee Shop.

■   Step 1 The first step in determining break-even is to separate fixed costs and variable costs.

Fixed costs include:

Advertising	$1,500
Insurance	1,000
Licences	450
Loan payments	2,000
Maintenance	750
Miscellaneous	350
Professional fees	1,250
Rent	6,000
Telephone	2,100
Utilities	3,600
Total fixed costs	19,000

These are the costs that Connie must pay before she sells a single cup of coffee. They are also known as her overhead.

Variable costs:

Payroll	$14,000
Inventory	11,000
Supplies	1,600
Total variable costs	26,600

■ Step 2 Calculate the variable cost percentage, determined as follows:

$$\text{Variable cost percentage:} \quad \frac{\text{variable cost}}{\text{revenues}} \quad : \quad \frac{26,600}{58,500} \quad : \quad 45\%$$

■ Step 3 Calculate the contribution margin: 100% − variable cost percentage: 100% − 45% = 55%

■ Step 4 Calculate break-even sales

$$\frac{\text{total fixed cost}}{\text{contribution margin}} \quad : \quad \frac{\$19,000}{.55} \quad : \quad \$34,545$$

That is Connie's break-even point in gross revenue. Another type of calculation could determine break-even on a unit basis instead of a dollar basis. This is very helpful in trying to quantify your sales and estimate whether you think your business can do sufficient volume. The steps to calculate break-even on a unit basis are as follows:

■ Step 1 Classify costs between fixed and variable.

■ Step 2 Calculate price per unit: $\dfrac{\text{total sales}}{\text{number of units sold}}$

■ Step 3 Calculate variable cost per unit: $\dfrac{\text{total variable cost}}{\text{total units sold}}$

■ Step 4 Calculate contribution dollars per unit: price per unit − variable cost per unit

■ Step 5 Calculate break-even in units =

$$\frac{\text{fixed costs}}{\text{selling price per unit} - \text{variable cost per unit}}$$

In the case of Connie's Coffee Shop, her fixed costs were $19,000, the coffee was $1.25 per cup and the variable costs were $.18 per cup. So break-even in units was

$$\frac{\$19,000}{1.25 - 0.18 =} \quad : \quad \frac{}{1.07} \quad 17,757 \text{ per year or 49 cups a day.}$$

Break-even analysis can be very powerful in quantifying the sales volumes necessary for your business. In this case, Connie was confident that she could sell 49 cups a day.

Jean Paul and Kathryn sat down to work through their initial capital requirements and their pro forma financial statements. They engaged in exhaustive research and obtained estimates from several builders and their architects in arriving at their initial capital requirements.

In addition, they were helped by a B&B owner who was happy to share the costs of his renovation. They also budgeted a contingency amount as well as working capital (see Table 11.2).

Although we will be discussing financing in the next chapter, for purposes of preparing the balance sheet, assume Jean Paul and Kathryn

TABLE 11.2   Chateau Orleans' initial capital requirement

Startup expense	Amount
1 Cost of building	$500,000
2 Renovations and improvements	$250,000
3 Professional fees	$ 5,000
4 Furniture and fixtures	$ 50,000
5 Inventory	$ 10,000
6 Office supplies and equipment	$ 5,000
7 Marketing and promotion	$ 12,500
8 Permits, licences and deposits	$ 7,500
9 Insurance	$ 5,000
10 Contingency	$ 50,000
11 Working capital	$ 75,000
Total	$970,000

will be borrowing $750,000 and raising $220,000 in equity. Their next step was to prepare a pro forma cash flow statement. They used several sources to determine projected revenues. One was the competitive matrix analysis that they prepared as part of their marketing plan. The next was information on the tourist market in New Orleans. The final component was pro forma financial statements that were used in the industry. They settled for occupancy rates 10 per cent below startups in their industry. In addition, they projected modest growth. They were also able to use pro forma percentages based upon the industry studies. In this way, their expenses and their revenues have a good correlation founded in historical data. They also factored in seasonal fluctuations with the tourist market in New Orleans. Their first year pro forma was as shown in Table 11.3.

TABLE 11.3 Chateau Orleans' pro forma financial statement

# of rooms	22	
Total available nights	8,030	
Occupancy	50%	
Total rooms occupied	4015	
Average daily rate	$55	
Revenues: room sales	$220,825	
Expenses:	Amount	% of total tevenue
Payroll	$30,915	14%
Marketing	22,083	10%
Booking fees	11,041	5%
Utilities/telephone	11,041	5%
Professional fees (actg/legal/ consulting)	6,625	3%
Repairs and maintenance	11,041	5%
Insurance/taxes	17,666	8%
Office expenses	2,208	1%
Other (laundry/miscellaneous)	6,625	3%
Supplies	13,250	6%
Loan repayment ($750,000 at 8%)	66,036	30%
Total expenses	$198,531	90%
Net cash flow	$22,294	10% (approximate)

However, before they did their annual pro forma, Jean Paul and Kathryn prepared monthly pro formas for the Chateau Orleans. Table 11.4 is an example of the monthly pro formas from January–March. Note the seasonal fluctuations. The beginning of the year is traditionally slow in the industry. However, business in February in New Orleans is very good due to the Mardi Gras holiday, which is a large tourist attraction.

TABLE 11.4   Chateau Orleans' monthly pro formas (Year 1)

	January	February	March
# of rooms	22	22	22
Total available nights	31	28	31
Occupancy	35%	70%	45%
Total rooms occupied	239	431	306
Average daily rate	$50	$65	$55
Revenues: room sales	$11,950	$28,015	$16,830
Expenses:			
Payroll	$1,673	$3,922	$2,356
Marketing	2,200	2,200	2,200
Booking fees	598	1400	347
Utilities/telephone	486	1,528	486
Professional fees (actg/ legal/consulting)	550	550	550
Repairs and maintenance	597	1,400	841
Insurance/taxes	1,472	1,472	1,472
Office expenses	184	184	184
Other (laundry/ miscellaneous)	504	1,850	504
Supplies	717	1,680	1,009
Loan repayment	5,503	5,503	5,503
Total expenses	$14,484	$21,689	$15,452
Net cash flow	$(2,534)	$6,326	$1,378

TABLE 11.5   Chateau Orleans' pro formas (Years 2 and 3)

	Year 2	Year 3
# of rooms	22	22
Total available nights	8,030	8,030
Occupancy	55%	60%
Total rooms occupied	4,416	4,818
Average daily rate	$57	$60
Revenues: room sales	$251,712	$289,080
Expenses:		
Payroll	$35,240	$40,471
Marketing	25,171	28,908
Booking fees	12,586	14,454
Utilities/telephone	12,586	14,454
Professional fees (actg/legal/ consulting)	7,551	8,672
Repairs and maintenance	12,586	14,454
Insurance/taxes	20,136	23,126
Office expenses	2,517	2,890
Other (laundry/miscellaneous)	7,551	8,672
Supplies	15,102	17,345
Loan repayment	66,036	66,036
Total expenses	$217,062	$239,482
Net cash flow	$34,650	$49,598

After preparing the pro forma cash flow statement, the next step is to prepare a pro forma balance sheet. This would be the pro forma balance sheet prepared as of the first day of operations.

As mentioned before, Jean Paul and Kathryn intend to finance the project with a loan of $750,00 and an equity infusion of $220,000. Note that the balance sheet can be prepared from the initial capital statement.

In examining the initial capital statement, the first step is to calculate out the assets. The assets are as follows:

ASSETS

Real property
   cost of building $500,000
   renovations and improvements $250,000
   total building   **$750,000**

Furniture and equipment
   furniture and fixtures $50,000
   equipment $5,000

Other assets
   inventory $10,000

Cash
   working capital $75,000
   contingency   50,000

Step 2 is to list your liabilities, which would be the costs payable. Assume that we have

Liabilities:
bank debt $750,000

FIGURE 11.4   Chateau Orleans' – pro forma balance sheet

Assets		Liabilities	
Current assets		Current liabilities	
Cash	$125,000		
Inventory	10,000		
Long-term (non-current assets)		Long-term (non-current) Liabilities	
Furniture and equipment	55,000	Bank debt (long-term)	$750,000
Property (bed and breakfast)	750,000		
		Owner's equity: original capital	190,000
Total assets	**$940,000**	**Total liabilites + owner's equity**	**$940,000**

Note: For purposes of simplicity, prepaid fees and costs of $30,000 (professional, marketing, permits and insurance) are not considered part of the pro forma balance sheet.

Summary

1   The first financial statement of the startup is the initial capital requirement. Carefully research to be sure that your initial capital requirements are both inclusive and accurate. Estimate adequate working capital.

3   The next financial statement for the startup is to estimate your pro forma cash flow statements, which involves estimating your revenue as well as expenses. Use your market research to determine and estimate revenue. Avoid straightlining your accounts and back up your numbers with research.

4   Divide your expenses into fixed and variable expenses. Use this to calculate break-even. Calculate break-even in dollars, which is fixed cost/contribution margin percentage. Then calculate break-even in terms of units = fixed costs/selling price − variable cost per unit.

Action step

■   Prepare the initial capital requirements for your business. Also prepare pro forma cash flow statements for 12 months, and then for three years. Prepare a pro forma balance sheet. Calculate your break-even point in terms of dollars and units.

■ CHAPTER TWELVE ■

Advanced accounting – financial analysis

We cannot direct the wind . . . But we can adjust the sails.

(Anon.)

Fundamentals of financial analysis

Now that we have examined your initial capital requirement and pro forma cash flow statements, then the next accounting application is to perform financial management with respect to your business. Financial management involves the review and analysis of your financial data to provide the basis for management decisions for your business. When you begin to think and act as a financial manager, you are taking that final step in 'financial literacy.' Like the financial managers at large companies, you are using your accounting tools to manage your business.

These tools will take you a step further in monitoring your 'financial vital signs.' Two of these tools include *comparisons* and *ratios*.

Comparisons

There are two ways to examine your financial position with comparisons. The first way is to compare your business with its own past performance. The second way is to compare your business with similar companies.

Comparing your business with its own past performance involves comparing your actual results with projected results. After carefully preparing the pro forma results in the previous chapter, you would want to then compare your operating results with your projections on at least a monthly, and possibly even a weekly, basis. Any deviation from your pro forma projections might require some investigation.

For example, suppose you are not meeting your revenue targets. Investigate to determine the problem. Is business generally down in your industry? Maybe you need to do more advertising or low-cost marketing. Perhaps your advertising is not reaching your target market. Maybe your initial revenue estimates were overly optimistic. In that case, you may need to quickly pare down your expenses. The comparison analysis can also be done on your expenses. Suppose your expenses are running higher than anticipated. Investigate. It could be due to a situation that is out of your control. Perhaps the costs have gone up in your industry. You might want to think about increasing your prices. But the increase in cost could be well within your control. You might need to tighten up operations.

The point in comparing projected results with actual results is to determine variations as they are occurring. You shouldn't wait until the end of the year to make comparisons. By then it might be too late to address any problems. The key to these types of comparisons is to use them on a monthly, weekly or even a daily basis. After a while, you will become very familiar with your business cycle and operations and will be able to determine very quickly whether there are any financial issues that need to be addressed.

The second step in using comparisons is to compare the actual results with those of the industry. One way to look at this is to calculate all of your costs as a percentage of net sales. In this manner, you can enter the percentages of total sales (revenues) that are standard for your industry. This is derived by dividing expenses items into your revenues and expressing them as a percentage of total net sales. In preparing the pro forma cash flow statement for Chateau Orleans, Jean Paul and Kathryn estimated their expenses based upon a percentage of revenue. They derived this information from industry sources in the B&B industry. Consequently, not only is their pro forma cash flow statement based on objective research, but it also provides them with an important basis for comparison. If the actual results of Chateau Orleans differ from the pro forma results, then the owners have both their estimated results and industry standards to use as a comparison. Consequently, any cost or revenue element that is out of line would require serious analysis. For example, suppose their payroll exceeds their projected amount. This would vary with their actual result. In addition, their payroll as a percentage of revenue would also vary with the industry standard. What this would tell them, quite emphatically, is that their payroll is out of line and that they need to do something about it.

These percentage amounts to be used for comparison can be obtained from various sources, such as trade associations, accountants or banks. The reference librarian in your nearest public library can refer you to documents that contain these industry percentage figures. In the

United States, an important source is Robert Morris & Associates' *Annual Statement Studies* (One Liberty Place, Philadelphia, PA 19103). Industry figures serve as a useful benchmark against which to compare cost and expense estimates that you develop for your business. Remember that one of the main purposes for using your financial measuring tools is to make management decisions with respect to your business. If you find through the use of comparisons that your revenue or costs are out of line for some reason, then it is important that you take steps to remedy the situation. Otherwise, you are not using these accounting tools to help your business

Ratios

Accounting ratios can serve as key indicators of financial performance and quickly highlight selected problems or issues with a business. Simply put, a ratio compares the relationship of one number to another. You are not really worried about the numbers in absolute terms, but rather in the relative terms of how the two numbers compare.

Ratios can quickly determine the fiscal health of your business. Since the numbers are relevant, ratios are accurate no matter what the size of the numbers involved. They can quickly diagnose problems and point out issues with the business. In addition, the ratios can be compared with previous operating results as well as with similar businesses.

The first set-up ratios of importance to the small business include those that measure short-term solvency of the business. These are ratios that bankers are going to be very concerned about. With cash and liquidity problems the leading causes of mortality for the small business, ratios on short-term solvency are particularly important.

Balance sheet ratios – measures of short term solvency

All of these ratios are dependent on the balance sheet. Once you have prepared your balance sheet, it is a quick process to fill the numbers into the ratio. For comparison's sake, let us consider the balance sheet of Connie's Coffee Shop. (see Figure 12.1)

FIGURE 12.1   Connie's coffee shop – balance sheet

Assets	=	Liabilities	+
Current assets		**Current liabilities**	
Cash	$20,000	Accounts payable	$ 1,000
Inventory	1,000		
Non-current assets		**Non-current liabilities**	
Equipment	3,000	Loan payable	$10,000
Computer	1,000		
		Owner's equity	$14,000
Total	$25,000	**Total**	$25,000

Quick ratio

This is the first ratio that we will consider, which is defined as follows:

$$\textbf{Quick ratio:} \quad \frac{\textbf{cash}}{\textbf{current liabilities}}$$

Referring back to the example of Connie's Coffee Shop, we remember that Connie's cash was $20,000 and her current liabilities were $1,000. In this case, Connie's quick ratio was $20,000 divided by $1,000, or 20. As you might expect, this would be considered a very high quick ratio. Usually, any quick ratio over 1 is considered to be very good. However, the ratios do depend on the particular industry and every industry is different. Other items that can come into the quick ratio include those that could be considered as cash equivalents. For example, marketable securities or accounts receivable can also be included in the numerator in computing your quick ratio.

Current ratio

The current ratio is closely related to quick ratio. To understand the current ratio, consider that assets and liabilities can be divided into two categories: *current* and *noncurrent*. Current assets are those that can be converted to cash in a year such as inventory and supplies. Noncurrent assets are those assets used in the longer term. This would include any machinery and equipment as well as your land or building. Current liabilities are those liabilities that are due within the year, such as your accounts payable. Your long-term liabilities are those payable over a longer term.

The current ratio is determined as follows:

$$\textbf{Current ratio:}\quad \frac{\textbf{current assets}}{\textbf{current liabilities}}$$

In the case of Connie's Coffee Shop, let us first determine her current assets. As is evident from her balance sheet, her current assets include the $10,000 in cash and the $1,000 in inventory. Equipment and machinery are not thought of as readily disposable assets and are therefore considered noncurrent. Since her current liabilities remain at $1,000, Connie's current ratio is 11, which is excellent. Since Connie has yet to accumulate much trade debt, her current and her quick ratio will remain high. They will drop as she accumulates more trade debt.

Debt to worth ratio

Bankers are generally interested in this type of ratio since it represents financial risk. The debt to worth ratio is determined as follows:

$$\textbf{Debt to net worth:}\quad \frac{\textbf{total liabilities}}{\textbf{owner's equity}}$$

As we discussed earlier, your owner's equity represents the net worth of your business. Therefore, this ratio measures the percentage of debt load for every dollar of net worth of the business. In the case of Connie, her liabilities total $11,000 and her owner's equity totals $14,000 giving her a debt to worth ratio of .78, which is very sound.

Income statement ratios – measures of performance

The next set of ratios pertain to the income statement. Remember that the income ratio is the dynamic part of the accounting equation, which is tied into financial performance.

Connie's Coffee Shop

FIGURE 12.2   Connie's coffee shop – cash flow statement

CONNIE'S COFFEE SHOP
CASH FLOW STATEMENT

Revenues			$58,500
Expenses			
	Advertising	$ 1,500	
	Insurance	$ 1,000	
	Inventory	$11,000	
	Licences	$ 450	
	Loan payments	$ 2,000	
	Maintenance	$ 750	
	Miscellaneous	$ 350	
	Payroll	$14,000	
	Professional fees	$ 1,250	
	Rent	$ 6,000	
	Supplies	$ 1,600	
	Taxes	$ 9,000	
	Telephone	$ 2,100	
	Utilities	$ 3,600	
Total expenses			45,600
Cash flow			$12,900

Net margin

The net margin of a business is calculated as follows:

$$\text{Net margin:} \quad \frac{\textbf{net profit}}{\textbf{revenue}}$$

The purpose of the net margin ratio is to measure profitability at the net profit level. It calculates the amount of net profit produced for every particular dollar of sales. In the case of Connie, the net margin would be $12,900/$58,500 or 22 per cent. That would also be considered healthy.

Asset utilization

This ratio measures the efficiency of the assets in generating sales.
The asset utilization ratio is calculated as follows:

$$\text{Asset utilization:} \quad \frac{\textbf{revenues}}{\textbf{total assets}}$$

In the case of Connie's Coffee Shop, the sales to total assets would be $58,500/$25,000, which is 2.34 to 1. This is also very good and many retail businesses that are not asset intensive would be considered as having a good asset utilization ratio. The important part of this ratio is to determine how the business utilizes its assets and whether the asset base is able to generate sufficient revenues for the business.

Return on assets

This ratio is similar to the asset utilization, but focuses on net income instead of revenue. The return on asset ratio is calculated as follows:

$$\text{Return on assets:} \quad \frac{\textbf{net income}}{\textbf{total assets}}$$

In Connie's case, it would be $12,900/$25,000 or 52 per cent, which is excellent.

Return on investment

This ratio determines the type of return that the owner is receiving for their investment in the business. The return on investment is calculated as follows:

Return on investment: $$\dfrac{\textbf{net profit}}{\textbf{owner's equity}}$$

In the case of our example, the return on owner's equity can be calculated as $12,900/$14,000 or 92 per cent.

Efficiency ratios

The next set of ratios for the business are also performance based. These are efficiency ratios designed to measure some of the specific operating data for the business. Note that some of these ratios, more specifically the inventory turnover ratio, will not be applicable for those businesses that have no inventory.

Accounts receivables turnover

This ratio measures the rate that your accounts receivable are being collected by the business. In our examples, we have used a cash business for simplicity, as well as to emphasize the importance of cash. However, it is quite possible that your business will be doing a lot of transactions on credit and that you will have significant accounts receivables. This ratio is important if you do have significant accounts receivable because it does determine the number of times that you can collect your accounts receivable. The accounts receivable turnover is determined as follows:

Receivables turnover: $$\dfrac{\textbf{revenues}}{\textbf{receivables}}$$

This is normally calculated on an annual basis. Usually, a higher number shows that your receivables are not out of line with regard to your sales.

Inventory turnover

The inventory turnover ratio measures the rate that inventory is used on an annual basis. It is calculated as follows:

Inventory turnover: $$\dfrac{\textbf{cost of goods sold}}{\textbf{inventory}}$$

For business in the retail industry, this inventory ratio is very critical. Generally, the higher the inventory turnover ratio the better, although an inventory ratio that is too high might indicate an inadequate amount of finished goods inventory or raw materials. An inventory ratio that is too low may indicate excessive finished goods or raw materials.

Cost cutting strategies

Note that sound financial management also includes cutting business costs (where possible). One of the goals of the business owner in cutting costs is to conserve cash and let others finance your business to the greatest extent possible. In suggesting this, I'm not advocating that you lean too much on your suppliers or engage in unethical business practices. Rather, I am suggesting that you always plan to preserve your cash. Manage your cash. Try to delay your payments as long as possible and obtain your receipts as soon as possible. Also, keep an eye out for any way that you can cut costs. Some ways are as follows:

Leases

One area to look at cutting costs might be with your lease. For those who signed a business lease, it might be the first time that you have done so and the business lease represents a new venture for you. Remember that the lease was written by the landlord with their interests in mind. The first item that I would recommend would be to carefully read your lease. Check the square footage. Many leases impose charges per square foot. If you find that your leased space is actually less than the square footage assigned, you might be owed a discount or a refund.

In larger office buildings, it might be useful to examine common area costs. Much of the costs imposed on leased premises consist of common area expenses assessed to the tenants. It is important to check these costs and to be sure that you're not paying an excess amount for the common area.

While we are discussing leases, do not be afraid to negotiate the terms of the lease, including rental rates and costs. Many people who sign a business lease for the first time readily agree to its provisions. They assume that the lease is non-negotiable because its terms are in writing. That is exactly what the landlord wants you to think. Anything is negotiable and that very much applies to business leases. Therefore, while you need to be aware of the market conditions, you also represent a revenue stream to the landlord. Try to negotiate lower rents in the early months of the lease while your business gets off the ground. If you are comfortable with your location and space, the landlord might make concessions in exchange for a longer-term lease.

Suppliers and customers

Another area where you can negotiate and cut costs is with your suppliers. Always request a prompt payment discount and determine the best terms for your suppliers. While you want to maintain a good relationship with a particular supplier or suppliers, don't feel compelled to stay with them. Remember, that one of the hallmarks of a good negotiator is being prepared. Regularly research your supply options to determine that you are receiving the best prices. Your objective is to obtain the best possible material for your costs. Don't ever let your supplier think that costs are no longer an issue. Always keep them honest in giving you the best possible price and look for ways that you can negotiate a reduction in the price.

Your customers are also an area where you can cut costs. Enquire about your customers paying a portion up front or a deposit with larger jobs. If the nature of your business requires considerable outlays on your part, perhaps part of these outlays can be paid for by the customer. As an attorney, I often request an advance from a new customer. A former law professor of mine always recommended obtaining an advance, claiming that it helps to clear the lawyer's mind. Also try to obtain your payments as quickly as possible.

Other areas to consider in cutting the cost of the business are your communications costs. The telecommunications industry is in a constant state of change, with more competitive packages being offered by different companies. But the telephone companies don't generally offer discounts unless they are requested. If you find out about a good offer from a competing company, call your provider and request a discount. Possibly switch to a competitor. Also negotiate your postage rates as low as possible. In addition, if your overnight volume is large enough, request a discount from major carriers.

Record-keeping strategies

Although record keeping is a chore, it is an important one. Maintaining good records can have the result of minimizing lost time in preparing financials and tax returns. We have already discussed the advantages of good records in keeping your accounting fees down. The types of records that you should consider for financial accounting and tax purposes include:

1   Business cheque book.

2   Supporting documents:

    (a)   Gross receipts: cash register tapes, bank deposit slips, receipt books, invoices.

    (b)   Purchases: cancelled cheques, cash register tapes.

    (c)   Expenses: cancelled cheques, cash register tapes.

3   Sample record system:

    (a)   Daily summary of cash receipts.

    (b)   Monthly summary of cash receipts.

    (c)   Cheque disbursements journal.

    (d)   Employee compensation record.

    (e)   Annual summary.

    (f)   Depreciation worksheet.

    (g)   Bank reconciliation.

Summary

1   After preparing the initial capital requirement and pro forma financial statements, the next step for the business owner is to use accounting tools for the financial management of their business.

2   Two important tools of the financial management function are comparisons and ratio analysis. Comparisons involve:

    (i)   comparing your actual results with expected results and;

    (ii)   comparing you actual results with those of the industry.

3   Be vigilant with both your cost-cutting and record-keeping strategy. Both of them will help you conserve cash and make your business life easier.

Action step

- If you have already generated some operating data, use comparisons and ratio strategies to analyse the data.

■ CHAPTER THIRTEEN ■

Fundamentals of financing your business: equity vs. debt

Great minds must not only be able to take opportunities,
but to make them.

(Colton)

The financing hurdle

The next step in making your business a reality is to secure adequate financing. Once you have determined your initial capital requirement (including working capital), your next step is to obtain the necessary funds. Often raising the money to finance the business poses the greatest hurdle to the entrepreneur. As we will see, many traditional sources of financing, such as bank financing, are going to be difficult for the startup to obtain. That's the bad news. But the good news is that there are many sources of non-traditional financing for the startup. With the entrepreneurial explosion in full swing, there are more ways to finance your business that ever before. In many areas, the government is becoming actively involved in helping to finance the small business. So while financing the startup can be difficult, it is certainly possible as long as you are prepared, creative and persistent.

Your first step in being prepared is to develop a (you guessed it!) BUSINESS PLAN. The first thing that prospective lenders and outside investors are going to ask to see is your business plan. A good business plan can be a tremendous help in securing your financing.

The second requirement for obtaining financing is being creative. Business startups are seldom financed from one source. Often their bootstrap financing comes from a multitude of sources including both debt and equity. The key is to be creative and use any source possible. I recently worked on a large entertainment facility that was financed with a mixture of bank debt, government loan guarantees, personal guarantees, privately raised equity, a line of credit and loans from the prospective suppliers of the business. This was a project which encountered several hurdles along the way. However, the principals were creative enough to look under every rock for money, including the *prospective suppliers of the business*. That's right, the principals approached their prospective suppliers for money, pointing out that the entertainment facility represented a potentially lucrative source of business for the suppliers. The suppliers agreed and actually loaned money to the project. It was this source of funds that put the project over the top. Now that's being creative!

The final requirement for obtaining financing is persistence or perseverance. We have already discussed perseverance as an essential trait of the entrepreneur. And nowhere can your perseverance be tested more than in trying to obtain financing.

Now we will discuss the different types of financing.

Debt vs. equity

There are basically two ways to finance a business, *debt* or *equity*. As you will discover, there are certain advantages and disadvantages of using debt and equity. Many businesses use a combination of both debt and equity. The key is to weigh their advantages and disadvantages and structure your business so that you have a proper mix of debt and equity.

Debt consists of those funds that you borrow to put into your business. Although debt comes in various shapes and sizes, the common element is that you owe the money and have to repay it. Naturally, the repayment terms are significant also. However, funds contributed as equity generally do not have to be repaid. Equity funds are contributed to the business in exchange for a certain part of the business. The equity investor receives ownership in your business and a share of its earnings. Most small businesses begin with an equity infusion by the owner. In fact many lenders or investors will not invest in a business in which the owner does not make an equity investment.

One way to consider the various impacts of debt and equity on your business is to return to our accounting equation of the balance sheet.

Equity

As Figure 13.1 indicates, the main advantage of equity is that it directly increases your owner's equity and gives a 'stronger' balance sheet. Your

FIGURE 13.1 Debt vs. equity impact on the balance sheet

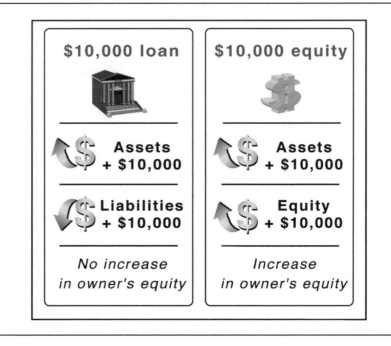

balance sheet ratios are better and your operations are not burdened with repayment. For the new business, an equity investment gives the business more breathing room as well as more room for debt in the future.

However, there are certain disadvantages to equity also. The first disadvantage is that outside equity investment is difficult to obtain. In fact, most equity contributions to the startup are made by the owner. Sometimes friends and family members will contribute also. Outside of this circle, raising equity funds becomes more difficult. In addition, raising money from outside investors triggers the application of laws regulating the purchase and sale of securities. Equity portions of a business are considered securities in most jurisdictions and are closely regulated. Your business attorney should be able to advise you in this area. Chapter 14 will discuss equity financing in more detail.

Another disadvantage of equity financing from outside sources is that you are relinquishing part of your business. Although you do not have a debt to repay, you are 'in effect' giving up a part of your business, and its percentage of assets and earnings, to an outside equity investor. The key is how much of the business do you have to give up in exchange for the equity financing? As we will discuss later, there is a certain breed of equity investors known as venture capitalists who specialize in funding startups, particularly in some of the technology businesses. But venture capitalists demand a large percentage of the equity interest, sometimes in the 40–60 per cent range. Consequently, the entrepreneur has to be careful about how much of the business they want to give up to equity investors. If your business ends up really taking off, then this initial equity financing could prove to be expensive.

Debt

There are advantages to debt also. The first advantage is that debt does not require that you give up part of your business. Once you repay the money, then you have no further obligation to your lenders. The second advantage is that some forms of debt, such as credit cards, can provide a quick and easy source of funds. Debt can be flexible and comes in many forms, from the conventional term loan to accounts receivable financing. Consequently, you can obtain a debt instrument that is carefully tailored to your operations. A final advantage of debt is that it is generally deductible for tax purposes.

Of course, debt also has its disadvantages. The first disadvantage is naturally that the debt has to be repaid and therefore constitutes a burden on your business. Debt can serve to hamper your operations if you incur too much of it. In addition, the terms of the debt can be costly to the business, with high interest rates. Any type of security interest on the debt can also serve as a hindrance to your operations.

That is why your business needs to be flexible in search of funds. As stated earlier, most businesses use a combination of debt and equity. While raising money is still difficult, there are more ways to finance a business than ever before. As the commercial lending industry continues to change, there are an increasing number of debt financing alternatives and sources available for the business. For example, a whole new lending market is springing up around accounts receivable financing, also known as factoring.

Financing sources

Next, we will discuss the various financing sources for your business. Some of them will be traditional while others will be non-traditional. In the next chapter, you'll find more details on developing a relationship with your banker, which is helpful to any financing strategy. In addition we will also talk about various equity raising strategies including the (gasp!) public offering.

Traditional sources

Self-financing

Self-financing by the owner is the most common form of financing for the small business startup. As mentioned earlier, most lenders and outside investors expect the owner to contribute a significant amount of funds to the business. In fact, if the owner doesn't think enough of the business to contribute funds, then it would be difficult to persuade others.

Naturally, everyone finds themselves in a different position with respect to their availability of funds. Your self-financing amount is a personal decision and depends upon you and your family's resources and obligations. Often the reality of the situation requires the owner to go into significant personal debt to finance the startup, which might even include mortgaging their house. In many cases, though, self-financing is not sufficient to sustain a business, and the owner has to seek outside capital. In fact, a prudent owner should secure adequate funds for their business before committing personal assets because it is much harder to obtain financing if the business should get into financial trouble. In other words, line up your money before you really need it.

Banks

Depending on who you talk to, banks can be either the best friend or worst enemy of the small business. Much has to do with the lending climate in your area. I have noticed that banks in the United States are becoming a little more friendly to the small business in recent years. But the situation may be different in your area. Despite your past success record with banks, I think it is important that you maintain as good a banking relationship as possible. A good banker can be a very important adviser to your business. I'll discuss the banking relationship in the next chapter.

Credit cards

Credit cards can be an important source of capital of the small business. Although many consider credit cards to be a non-traditional financing source, the use of credit cards to finance business startups is becoming more frequent and accepted. The list of businesses whose business startup was financed by credit cards range across the board and include the likes of Intuit, the manufacturer of the best selling personal financial software called Quicken. However, there is a very important caveat in dealing with credit cards, which is to be careful. Credit cards can be very dangerous. I've even heard them described as 'plastic heroin', just as alluring as the narcotic, but also addictive and dangerous. However, just as credit cards are responsible for record consumer debt in the world, they can also be a quick, easy way to obtain money for the growing business. Another advantage of credit cards is that they are generally secure and can be safeguarded against loss and theft.

The disadvantages of credit cards include the fact that the interest rate is usually high and they can get you into trouble very quickly. The key to using credit cards is to manage your credit card debt, just like you would any other debt. First, keep track of your credit card debt. Next, be sure to make minimum payments on the debt. Concentrate your debt on the cards paying the lower interest rate. As the cash flow from your business increases, you would want to increase your payments on the cards. The key is to take control of your credit card debt, rather than allowing it to control you and your business.

While credit cards can provide a source of ready capital for the small business, the key is to be careful and to use credit cards judiciously.

Government agencies

For some businesses, government agencies can be an important source of financing. In the United States, the Small Business Administration has emerged as an important source of capital. With its variety of programmes and loan guarantees, the administration has done much to help small business. Depending upon where you are located, your national or local government might have loan guarantees and pro-grammes directed to help the small business. You never know until you ask. You might want to begin with your local or regional department of economic development. Many government agencies have not only loan assistance, but professional and technical assistance to help the small business.

Venture capitalists

Venture capitalists are responsible for a considerable amount of business growth. Venture capitalists inject money into promising projects in return for a significant equity position or even control in some cases. However, just as there are good and bad in every industry, the same applies to venture capitalists. Be sure that your professional advisers are involved in your dealings with them, as there are many unscrupulous venture capitalists out there. Be wary of any venture capitalist or investment banker who requests money up front to find additional sources of money. As with any professional, you must check out the references of the venture capitalist.

Investment bankers

Somewhat related to venture capitalists are investment bankers. Usually, the investment bankers do not invest in your company themselves but rather secure funds for you from outside investors or lenders – for a fee. Although most businesses have to be at a mature stage before using investment bankers, it is never too early to think about the larger debt and equity markets to which the investment bankers have access.

The investment banker would generally be interested in those businesses in the technology field or other areas involving innovative products that have the capability of being mass produced on a significant basis and generating returns to the investors. Unless your business has that type of profit potential, most investment bankers are not going to be interested. You also need to exercise caution in your dealings with investment bankers. While many are from large and reputable firms, there are other shady operations under the guise of investment banking. As with venture capitalists, be wary of anyone who wants their fee up front to secure you additional money. Many of these 'financing fees' have never been repaid or led to anything else.

One of the ways that the investment banker raises money for the business is to take the business 'public.' As someone who has worked on a variety of public offerings, let me assure you that this is a massive undertaking. A public offering is geared only for a company that is either mature or has demonstrated profit potential. In addition, the public offering can be a very expensive process, involving hundreds of thousands or even millions of dollars in up-front fees.

Other lenders

Besides banking institutions, there are numerous other lending institutions, which could include credit unions, savings institutions and other lenders which lend money to business. In the last few years, an entire industry has arisen around lending upon accounts receivable. The term 'factoring' has become a new way to finance your receivables. As with a type of receivables, this would allow the owner to generate cash from the receivables. While the terms might vary, this could be attractive to the owner depending upon their circumstances.

Non-traditional sources

Although the rapidly evolving economy is quickly serving to blur the distinction between traditional and non-traditional sources, the following are some additional sources of capital for your business that are considered non-traditional.

Friends and family

Many business startups rely on the resources from friends and family members. These resources could be in the form of debt or equity contributions. Although turning to your family and friends might involve some humility, they can be a very important, and perhaps the only available, source of funds for your business. So ask! But deal with them at arm's length and prepare promissory notes and/or stock certificates as evidences of their contribution.

Angels

As their name might suggest, angels are those investors who invest in businesses for motivations that are sometimes more noble than just making money. The angel network consists of retired executives, philanthropists and other investors who have a desire to assist businesses. Although the angel is not looking to *give* their money away, they are definitely influenced by causes that they find worthy. Sometimes, angels invest in businesses in which they are interested. Other times they're looking to help worthy entrepreneurs.

   In trying to locate angel investors, be aware that there are many types out there. Some angel investors already own and operate a highly successful business of their own, but might be interested in other opportunities. Sometimes, they are interested in a business related to their own so that they can diversify their own investment portfolio. Other angels might be retired executives or entrepreneurs looking for something to do with their time and money. Usually, this type of angel would not want an active part in the business. Some other angels might include high earning professionals who would consider investing in a business with a product or service that they have some connection with. They might use the product in their business or be aware of it. Finally, as mentioned earlier, some angels just want to help worthy entrepreneurs. Perhaps you can come up with some type of social, ethnic or educational affiliation with that type of angel.

Private placements

Although the laws regulating the investment of funds differ around the world, the private placement can generally be thought of as a public offering on a smaller scale. Although the private placement is less complicated to prepare than the public offering, there are certain restrictions on the manner in which the offering can be advertised and investors solicited.

Customers

I discussed customer financing in the previous chapter when I spoke about conserving your cash. Don't be afraid to request advance payment or even a down payment in those industries where production takes several months.

Suppliers – commercial credit

The types of financing that you can obtain from your suppliers include the traditional commercial credit account. This involves the vendors delivering goods and services before payment is received. A good cash management strategy is to request either credit terms or a discount for prompt payment. Remember your goal is to conserve your cash and collect your money as quickly as you can, but take as long as possible to pay it back.

Joint ventures/strategic partnerships

Joining forces with another party can be a way to help finance all or part of your business. One possibility is to form a joint venture for a particular project with each party agreeing to finance a share. The joint venture could also be used to help finance your entire business needs. In this way, the joint venture would be very similar to a partnership. Another type of financing is to form a strategic partnership with another, sometimes larger company with which you have a commercial relationship. Sometimes the larger companies will agree to finance the smaller companies that produce necessary products or services that they use.

Sale of distribution rights

This is a somewhat exotic method of financing, in which businesses with a unique product or method raise money by selling their distribution rights to others. This is similar to a franchise, where the franchisor is paid fees and royalties for licensing its business method. However, the franchise relationship is generally more involved than a simple sale of distribution rights. The sale of distribution rights might apply in the situation where the franchise has yet to be formed or for the owner who does not want to franchise its operations.

Royalty financing

This is another exotic form of financing. Royalty financing can be thought of as an advance against future sales. In exchange for advancing the business money, the investors would be paid a certain percentage of sales or royalty. As opposed to receiving a percentage of the profits or bottom line, the investors would take their percentage from the revenues or the top. Should the business meet its sales targets, the investors would be rewarded. The owners have their original equity preserved and the investors receive funds from the business immediately. In addition, most securities laws do not apply to royalty financing. However, royalty financing might not be good for the business whose margins are too thin to support the payment of the percentage of royalties on revenues. Your royalty obligation would be just like any other expense.

Like most new businesses, Jean Paul and Kathryn's search for finance is anything but easy. They sign a purchase agreement on the property for $500,000, which gives them 60 days to secure financing. They are rejected by no fewer than six banks, who insist on at least 20 per cent equity in the project. Their search for equity capital is frustrating also. Their capital needs include approximately $750,000 in debt as well as $220,000 in equity. The two contribute their entire savings of $45,000, $10,000 of which was placed as a deposit on the property. Kathryn is able to borrow another $30,000 from her deferred savings plan. An aunt of Jean Paul gives him $30,000 against a future inheritance. The two are able to find six investors, who are Garden District residents themselves, to contribute $10,000 apiece. When Kathryn's father hears how close they are to raising the money, he contributes the remaining $45,000. With their equity raised, the two are finally able to get a bank loan of $750,000, which was guaranteed by the Small Business Administration. The loan is approved on the 58th day of signing the purchase agreement, and the sale closed 10 days later after the purchase contract was extended.

Summary

1   Financing your business is often the biggest hurdle for the startup. The key to obtaining your financing is to be prepared, creative and persistent.

2   There are two ways to finance your business: debt and equity. There are advantages and disadvantages to both. Most businesses are started with a mix of debt and equity.

3   Traditional sources of financing include banks, commercial institutions, credit cards and investment bankers. Non-traditional sources of financing include customers' suppliers and friends and family. The more potential sources of financing that you can locate, the more likely it is that you will be able to raise your necessary funds.

Action step

■   Make a list of all of the potential sources of funds for your business. Remember the key to obtaining finance is to be creative and persistent. Think of all possible sources of funds that you can obtain. Once you've made your list, get started! We will be discussing banks in greater detail in the next chapter.

CHAPTER FOURTEEN

Advanced finance – your banker and beyond

The surest way to go broke is to sit around and wait for a break.

(Anon.)

Your banker – the love/hate relationship

My clients and students generally either love or hate their banker. Some credit their banker with a great deal of their success while others think their banker is holding back their operations. Others are so frustrated by their inability to get bank financing, that they vow to never use a bank. One of my clients used a spinoff of John Gray's bestseller, *Men Are From Mars, Women Are From Venus* to describe his relationship with his banker. In case you have not heard of the book, it is a well-known guide which explains the fundamental differences between men and women and the way these differences need to be understood in achieving better relationships. My client also thinks that there are also fundamental differences between entrepreneurs and bankers. He describes the situation as 'Entrepreneurs Are From Mercury and Bankers Are From Pluto' or perhaps even 'Uranus', depending upon your opinion of your banker.

Actually, bankers are not that bad. It's my experience that banks have become fairly accommodating to the small business. For example, some bankers are even looking beyond the loan collateral and considering the knowledge and ability of the business owner.

Despite the size of your business or your readiness to obtain bank financing, you would be well served by at least establishing a relationship with a banker. The banking relationship can be very important in financing the later growth and development of your business. Like your attorney and accountant, your banker can emerge as a very important part of your entrepreneurial team and assist you in growing your business. A good banker can not only find the best sources of capital to finance your business, but can also help you manage your business. The banker reviews financial statements all day long and in some cases may even advise businesses that are similar to yours. Other than the fees or interest that you pay on the loan, the advice from your banker is free. In other words, you can really leverage your banker to provide financial advice about your business. However, don't waste your banker's time – only contact them when you are serious about establishing a banking relationship either presently or in the near future. However, like any relationship, your relationship with your banker works both ways and does involve some give and take. You need to devize a strategy in order to deal with and cultivate a fruitful association with your banker.

Before the entrepreneur can get the bank to understand them, they have to understand the bank. According to Melissa Moffatt Elliott of Hibernia National Bank in New Orleans, the most important thing that business startups must keep in mind is that unlike the entrepreneur, *banks are not risk takers*. Melissa specializes in small business banking and recently won an award for small business lending. She emphasized that, unlike venture capitalists, banks have to comply with stringent regulatory requirements and are therefore looking for the 'safe' loans. These 'safe' loans are generally secured with solid cash flow and collateral. The first priority is a source of cash flow to repay the loan. For the startup without cash flow, the bank might accept a secondary source of cash flow such as a working spouse or a relative who co-signs the note. In addition, readily identifiable collateral such as real estate or securities would also be required.

In looking to make loans to the existing business, the history of the business is very important. A business with a solid cash flow has a much better chance of receiving a loan. The banks also are very interested in the hard financial numbers or ratios, similar to those discussed in Chapter 12. One ratio relied on by banks is the *debt repayment to cash flow* ratio. This ratio measures the total amount of the debt divided by the cash flow of the business. According to Melissa, the bank wants a ratio of $1.4 of cash flow to every $1 of debt repayment. But in the case of the startup business with no cash flow, there is the possibility of looking to other sources of income, such as a spouse who is working. Other items considered by the bank include whether the monthly total for debt payments is in excess of 45 per cent of the income. Items that help the credit scoring include a solid credit history, a low debt ratio and current assets. Naturally any type of government subsidy such as a loan guarantee would help soften up the criteria.

Melissa emphasized that a good business plan was very important also. Although the entrepreneur might not have particular experience in that industry, they could demonstrate superior knowledge with a carefully thought out business plan. She also cautioned that the startup costs of the business needed to be carefully estimated and that banks are very hesitant to lend if the owner does not put any of their own money into the business. If the owner does not have enough faith in the business to help fund it, how can the bank be expected to have faith in the business?

Other bankers I spoke with agreed that a well-prepared business plan is very important. It is helpful if the pro forma cash flows are based upon differing operating scenarios. For example, suppose the amount of business is less than anticipated or some costs run higher. By thinking through various contingencies, the entrepreneur can better prepare the business for the unexpected, and perhaps budget more working capital. Cash flow rather than book income should be the focus of the financial projections and prospective borrowers should obtain as much information as possible from similar businesses.

FIGURE 14.1 Dealing with your banker

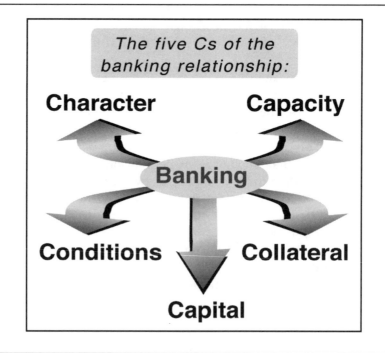

Dealing with your banker

Now that we have examined how bankers think, the following are some tips in dealing with your banker. In the banking industry, this relationship is referred to as the five Cs, which are as follows:

Character

Your banker wants someone that they can trust. While the banker will be interested in the financial information of your business, they are also interested in *you* because they are lending the money to *you*. Don't do anything to damage the trust between you and your banker. Be honest and up-front. Don't make promises that you cannot keep. If something adverse happens to your business, notify your banker immediately.

Capacity

Your capacity for borrowing is based upon your financial strength and your track record. If you're just starting out in business, your borrowing capacity will be limited. The key is to initiate a banking relationship and then to build capacity. Once you have a longer track record and you increase your business, you'll be able to borrow more. Although credit cards can be a source of cash, one thing to remember is that unused credit cards may affect your borrowing capacity. Therefore, if you have an existing banking relationship or anticipate one in the future, cut down on excess credit cards. This is particularly true for cards that you don't use in the business.

Capital

The bank is going to want other capital invested in the venture besides theirs. This would include the funds of the owner. While this might require some sacrifice and risk on your part, the bank wants to see that you are confident in your business. Consequently, as mentioned earlier, be prepared to sink some of your own money into your business if you are serious about bank financing.

Collateral

As was stated earlier, banks are not risk takers. Therefore, they're going to require some collateral to support their primary source of repayment. Many are offended by this, but collateral is a simple fact of the banking industry. You could later try to negotiate the release of the collateral, should the cash flow of the business adequately service the debt. However, at the beginning of a banking relationship, be prepared to furnish some collateral to secure the loan.

Conditions

The final aspect in dealing with your banker concerns the prevailing economic and business conditions prevalent in the area as well as your industry. Prevailing economic conditions affect everyone and can be a large part of the credit equation. Loans are simply more difficult to make during bad economic times than in good economic times.

Preparing a loan request

One of the advantages in preparing a business plan is that it gives you much, if not all, of the data that you need to prepare a loan request. Like the business plan, the loan request requires that you describe the history and nature of your business and your management team, as well as general information about your products or services. For example, you would include your market, major customers, suppliers and competition. You would also include your key advisers such as your accountant, attorney, commercial insurance agent and other members of your team.

Items on the loan request include:

- the purpose of the loan;
- the amount requested;
- the desired term;
- the source of repayment;
- available collateral.

The financial information that is required in the loan request includes:

- three years of financial statements and tax returns, for your business and for you individually;

- ratio analysis: which includes debt service coverage, current ratio and debt to equity;

- annual budget;

- sources and uses of cash.

When making the loan, the lender goes through a process known as credit analysis whereby the lender decides whether or not the loan is likely to be paid. There are essentially two tests that the lender uses in the credit analysis process. The first test is the liquidity test, in which the lender determines whether or not there will be sufficient cash from internal operations to pay interest and to amortize the debt. The ratios that are involved in the liquidity tests are very similar to the ratios used in earlier chapters on efficiency. In addition, the lender also uses a solvency test to determine if there is sufficient cash from other sources, primarily the company assets, to pay interest and amortize the debt.

Creative equity financing

The other type of financing is equity financing, which involves the sale of equity or ownership interest in the business. In the previous chapter, we discussed some of the advantages of equity financing. Since the equity funds do not have to be repaid, they can represent a powerful cash infusion into the business which strengthens operations as well as the balance sheet.

Some of the more publicized equity financings involve public offerings in the high tech sector, sometimes transforming entrepreneurs into millionaires (sometimes even billionaires) practically overnight. Although such dramatic results are rare, equity financing is a viable alternative for many businesses. I have had some success in raising money for businesses with private placements. A private placement involves an exemption from the public offering registration, allowing businesses to raise money 'privately' from a small pool of individual investors. The private placement does involve the preparation of a private placement memorandum furnishing all material information, including audited financial statements. In addition, there are restrictions on the manner and sale of private offerings and other filing and compliance regulations. Private placements are responsible for a fair amount of capital raised for businesses. However, there is legal liability involved and private placements need to be done carefully.

There are many elements involved in developing a strategy for outside equity financing. Since we saw that banks are not risk takers, some businesses have to step beyond traditional barriers and look to equity financing. This is particularly true for those business startups that might be thought of as inherently risky. Unlike banks, venture capitalists or professional investors are used to considerable risks. In fact, many of these investors know at the outset that they will lose on most of their investments. However, it is that one or two out of 10 which are very profitable that makes it all worth their trouble.

As discussed earlier, the businesses that have the best chance for equity financing are those in a high-growth area. Businesses with small target markets are not particularly good candidates for equity investment on a large scale. This is not to say that the local restaurant will not be able to obtain backing from local investors. But professional investors are not going to be particularly interested. Perhaps the owner of a local business could generate some interest by demonstrating the potential to expand their local concepts to a larger market. But since equity investors are taking a greater risk, they want a greater return for that risk. You need to be able to convince investors of a good return down the line.

The first thing an outside investor is going to want to see is your business plan. They will want to know what exactly your company does. This is the opportunity to provide them with your 'sizzle'. It is often the sizzle of the company which helps to sell the company to equity investors.

Adequate financing for high-growth potential businesses is a critical ingredient in their survival. In most cases this need for outside capital is a very positive indicator of the success of the business. Although your company may be just starting, a proactive look for equity investment is not a waste of time. I spoke earlier about leveraging your attorney and your accountant. Perhaps they might have clients who are interested in investing. I have put some of my legal clients in touch with professional investors. Also begin making contacts in the investment community in your area.

A detailed capital search programme should include a specifically targeted list of potential investors. When I am contacted by a potential client to prepare a private placement memorandum, the first thing I ask is whether they have a target list of investors. Since the costs of the private placement are not low, I recommend that they have a definite strategy to sell their equity interest. The only way that their private placement memorandum will be worthwhile is if they can sell sufficient portions of equity to adequately cover the legal and accounting costs. This target list would include those acquaintances who believe in their ability and who are interested in the project. The list could also include any number of investors, from angels to professional investors.

Some aspects of your business that outside investors are going to be interested in include the following:

Exit strategy

Most investors want to know how they are going to get their money out of the deal. They are generally not interested in long-term investments. They will want to know whether you intend to either go public or to sell the business down the road.

Return on investment

All investors are interested in the amount of return on their investment. Higher risk investments generally expect a greater return. This return should not only be higher than that offered by banks but also other equity investments, such as publicly traded companies on the stock market. This is because there's greater risk.

Technology

As mentioned earlier, one thing that would quickly attract investor attention is the potential for a breakthrough in technology which would allow your products or services to dominate a market. If you can satisfactorily demonstrate this, then you will have no trouble raising money.

Superior value

Even if your business is not in the technology area, you still have a chance to attract investor attention by demonstrating superior value. For example, does your firm represent a superior value to the investor on the basis of some superior feature? Are your costs minimal? Can your business expand dramatically to meet demand? Is there sufficient cash flow and a strong enough balance sheet to support expansion?

If you have appealing enough factors, the next step is to target those investors who are more likely to invest in your type of business. Since not all investors are interested in all investment opportunities, you need to tailor the opportunity to the different investor. What will be the aspects about your business that will be of interest to the particular investors? What are they looking for in an investment? Are they looking more for capital appreciation? Community participation? Ego gratification? The programme for raising capital will differ depending on whether you have high-growth potential, something which could be ego satisfying such as a restaurant or entertainment-related facility, or a community service type of a business.

For example, if your investment is an entertainment facility, you might target high-earning professionals in the area who might be interested in such an 'ego investment.' As opposed to rate of return, they might be more interested in being able to say that they are a part owner of the facility. For the high-tech business with great capital needs, you are going to have to target professional investors and angels. For a retail dress shop catering to professional women, you might target your potential customer base for part ownership. The key is to figure out what the investment opportunity represents to the investor. People who are community oriented might be willing to invest in your movie theatre which converts an abandoned building and helps to revitalize an area. Maybe your investor could benefit from your activity. Perhaps the owner of a coffee shop chain might be interested in investing in your coffee bean roasting operation.

As we have discussed earlier, there are many different types of investors. We've already discussed angels in some detail. As you know, angels do represent a wide range of values and your job is to match your business with their values. Other types of investors could directly benefit from your business. This would include your employees, managers, customers and suppliers, who depend on the operation of your business. There is also a class of wealthy individuals or professionals looking to broaden their sphere of activity. These people are similar to the entrepreneurial angels, but have significant resources and self confidence to make them desirable as potential investors.

In summary, it is possible to raise private equity capital provided that your business offers something of particular interest to the investor and you are able to target the particular investor.

Public offerings

Some might consider it a bit premature to even discuss public offerings in a book that is primarily geared to new and startup businesses. However, as I will discuss in Chapter 19, it is important that every business has a harvest strategy. Since all good things must come to an end, begin with the end in mind.

The public offering can be an excellent harvest strategy. Not only does it place a market value on the owner's business, but it also provides an efficient mechanism for the owner to sell all or part of their business. Consequently, a public offering could very well be a goal for your business. Most of the large public companies of the world were once small, privately held companies, just like yours. There's no reason why you should limit your own future.

With that said, do note that the expense and time associated with a public offering is considerable. Depending on the prevailing securities laws in your area, the public offering will require a very definite commitment of resources, both in time as well as professional fees. Typically, the public offering is focused around the preparation of a registration statement to be filed with the proper authorities. The registration statement is very detailed and provides a great deal of information about your business. In fact, some parts of the registration statement are very similar to the business plan. There is much accounting information required. An accountant and attorney specializing in securities matters are the key advisers in the preparation of the registration statement. The other important professional is the investment banker, who will underwrite the public offering. The investment banker generally handles the structuring of the offering, including pricing and its distribution to the public.

Some of the items of information contained in the public offering are as follows:

The company

Exact corporation name, state and date of incorporation, street address of principal office, company telephone number, fiscal year, and the name of the person to contact at the company with respect to the offering.

Introductory statement

The objective of this statement is to summarize items for potential investors. This summary includes:

1   Risk factors: the factors which the company considers to be the most substantial risks to an investor in this offering.

2   Business and properties: a general description of the business and properties of the company, which is very similar to the business plan, and would address such areas as:

    (a) products or services;

    (b) the industry in which the company is selling, or expects to sell, its products or services;

    (c) competition;

    (d) current or anticipated prices or price ranges for the company's products or services, or the formula for determining prices;

    (e) marketing strategies;

    (f) employees;

    (g) principal properties (such as real estate, plant and equipment, patents, etc.,) which the company owns.

3   Use of proceeds: set forth the use of the proceeds from this offering, e.g. expansion, working capital, etc.

4   Capitalization: indicate the capitalization of the company as of the most recent balance sheet date and as adjusted to reflect the sale of the minimum and maximum amount of securities in this offering and the use of the net proceeds therefrom.

5   Description of securities: describe the characteristics of the securities, whether they are stock, debt or another form of security.

6   Financial statements: reviewed or audited financial statements for the last fiscal year need to be attached.

7   Management's discussion and analysis of certain relevant factors: describe any trends in the company's historical operating results. If the company's financial statements show losses from operations, explain the causes underlying these losses and what steps the company has taken or is taking to address these causes. Indicate any changes now occurring in the underlying economies of the industry or the company's business.

Summary

1   Your banker can be as important an adviser to your business as your attorney and your accountant. Seek to develop a commercial banking relationship as soon as possible.

2   Some tips in dealing with your banker include being honest and well prepared and having a good business plan. Although lending is mostly a financial decision, your character and knowledge can play an important part in tipping the balance in your favour.

3   For some businesses with the potential for high growth, or which represent a value to investors, a good equity search strategy can be helpful. Focus your search for private equity capital on those investors who would have the most interest in investing in your business.

Action steps

- Determine the proper mix of debt and equity for your business.

- Follow the steps discussed above in seeking debt and/or equity financing.

CHAPTER FIFTEEN

Putting it all together – your business plan

The difference between ordinary and extraordinary is that little bit extra.

(Anon.)

Your business plan

In the previous chapters, we have discussed all of the material that you will need to prepare your business plan. The remaining chapters will focus on items such as alternative entry strategies, self-management techniques and technology use by the small business. As the above quotation indicates, the only real difference between an ordinary business plan and an extraordinary plan is that little bit extra that you put into the business plan. With each detail that your research uncovers, each problem that you are able to work through and each assumption that you can validly determine, your business plan grows clearer and more helpful to you. As your business plan becomes clearer, then so does the focus of your business and your ultimate results.

No one ever said that the writing of a business plan is an easy process. As is evident from the previous chapters, it can be a tedious and somewhat complicated process. But it is one that needs to be done. Below is a final review of the parts of the business plan. Compare the checklist against your plan to be sure that you've covered everything. Also, do that little bit extra and make your business plan extraordinary.

Business plan checklist

I Cover page and TOC

II Executive summary/statement of purpose

1   Overview of your business.

2   Short description of your product or service, market, industry.

3   Your vision for the business. What are your goals for the business? Why is your business distinctive? What is your overall strategy for competing in the market?

III Management and organization

1   Legal issues

   (a) Form of business. What form will your business be: sole proprietorship, partnership, corporation, limited liability company?

   (b) Intellectual property: whether your business has any significant issues with respect to intellectual property. Is the intellectual property adequately protected?

   (c) Required licences or permits. Are there necessary licences for the business?

   (d) Significant regulation of business. Any significant regulatory requirements?

   (e) Any pending litigation?

2   Professional advisers:

   (a) attorney;

   (b) accountant;

   (c) commercial insurance agent;

   (d) banker;

   (e) consultants – marketing, human resources, business broker;

   (f) board of advisers.

IV Description of product or service

1 Description of business

   (a) Business type: merchandising, manufacturing or service.

   (b) What your product or service is. What you are selling. Emphasize its uniqueness. Unique selling proposition (USP).

   (c) Is it a new independent business, a takeover, an expansion?

   (d) Why your business will be profitable. What are the growth opportunities?

   (e) When your business will be open (days, hours).

   (f) What you have learned about your kind of business from outside sources (trade suppliers, bankers, publications).

   (g) Description of the benefits of your goods and services from your customers' perspective. Successful business owners know or at least have an idea of what their customers want or expect from them.

   — How your product or service will benefit the customer.

   — Which products/services are in demand; if there will be a steady flow of cash.

2 The location of your business. Note that the location of the business can play a decisive role in its success or failure.

3 Competition:

   (a) Who are your direct competitors? Prepare a competitive matrix analysis. Compare your business on the basis of price, quality, features, uniqueness, amenities, selection, business condition, strengths/weaknesses, facilities, location.

   (b) Who are your indirect competitors?

   (c) What have you learned from their operations? From their advertising?

IV Marketing plan

1   Customer profile – know your customer.

(a)   Age, sex, socioeconomic status, behaviour, likes, dislikes.

(b)   Describe the profile of your customer(s)

2   Market segmentation.

(a)   Describe the target market of your business.

(b)   Describe the types of market segmentation variables, psychographic, behavioural, demographic and geographic that are relevant.

3   Fundamentals of your marketing mix.

(a)   Product: how are you going to market the uniqueness of your product or service?

(b)   Place: the distribution of your product or service. Relevant factors about your location.

(c)   Price: the pricing strategy for your business. State whether you will use any type of pricing strategy, such as penetration pricing.

(d)   Promotion: discuss the type of promotion strategy that you will use. What type of advertising will you use? What is your budget and timetable for the advertising? You could use the worksheet at the end of Chapter 7.

— direct mail;

— print advertising;

— media;

— Internet;

— low cost marketing;

— public relations.

VI Financial data

1 Prepare the statement of initial capital requirement.

2 Pro forma cash flow statement on a monthly basis for one year, two additional years.

3 Pro forma balance sheet.

4 Financing plan: what mix of debt and equity will be used in your business?

VII Conclusion

VII Appendices

1 Tax returns of principals for last three years.

2 Personal financial statement (all banks have these forms).

3 Copy of proposed lease of purchase agreement for building space.

4 Copy of licences and other legal documents.

5 Copy of résumés of all principals.

6 Copies of letters of intent from suppliers, etc.

7 Any advertising or promotional material.

PART III

Beyond the business plan

CHAPTER SIXTEEN

Other market entry strategies – franchising and buying a business

There is no future in any job. The future lies in the man who holds the job.

(George Crane)

There are ways of owning your own business without starting it yourself. One way is to buy an existing business. The purchaser of an existing business is seeking to bypass the sometimes time consuming and involved process of establishing and building a business. Ideally, the purchaser is hoping to be able to build from someone else's efforts. Another market entry strategy is to purchase a business prototype or a franchise. Franchising has experienced a boom in recent years as people with no business experience of their own contract to use someone else's prototype.

However, while buying a business or a franchise can provide a certain shortcut to ownership, don't take any short cuts in evaluating either business opportunity. In fact, many of the business planning techniques that we have discussed in the book will help you analyse an existing business or a franchise opportunity.

Franchising

What is a franchise?

Franchising involves a contractual relationship between a franchisor and a franchisee. The franchisor is the owner of a particular service or product. The *franchisee* is interested in offering the product or service in a particular market. The *franchise* is the exclusive right to offer that product or service in a particular market. In return for granting that particular business opportunity for the local distribution, the franchisor receives a payment and/or royalty from the franchisee.

Take, for example, a typical fast-food franchise. In this case, the franchisee has contracted with the franchisor to offer the food products of the franchisor in a particular market. The agreement will also require the franchisee to conform with quality standards. This type of agreement would be a business format franchise, which is one of the more popular forms of franchises today. In this case, the franchising goes beyond a particular product and assumes a contractual, ongoing business relationship between the franchisor and the franchisee. In addition, the franchisor supplies the franchisee with many documents, which include a procedures manual and a marketing plan. The franchisor can also provide assistance with the business development. The business format franchise is a more complex way of franchising in that it involves the sale of an overall way of doing business as opposed to the rights to distribute a product.

Payments for the franchise opportunity range from relatively modest payments to hundreds of thousands of dollars to build out the franchise operations. One way to view a franchise opportunity is a way of decreasing risk. You are decreasing your risk in the particular business by buying the franchisors's know-how and their business methodology in setting up your business.

The number of franchises is increasing dramatically throughout the world. New opportunities and innovation in certain computer software, environmentally safe products and even bagel making have been emerging. In addition, some hard-fought battles to ease the imbalance of power between franchisors and franchisees have had some effect. Also, some franchisees have been beefing up their encroachment policies to guarantee the franchisees more territorial protection. In the United States, there have been more disclosures required by franchisors, such as complete details about past litigation against the franchisor, supplier rebates, computer systems, revenues, and training programmes.

Is a franchise for me?

One of the first questions you might want to consider is whether you have the right personality to be a franchisee. In the case of the business format franchise, you're not exactly your own boss. While you do run your franchise operations, they are run according to the detailed specifications of the franchisor. Consequently, if you value and like to exercise your own creativity in running a business, then a franchise might not be for you. However, if you don't mind implementing what someone has set out for you, then a franchise might be good. It is a personal decision that also depends on whether you value the product or service and how much you wish to get involved.

Evaluating the franchise

The first item to consider is whether the particular business is for you. Are you impressed with the idea or products that the franchisor is offering? Can you see yourself offering these products or services for some time? If your honest answer is yes, then you can proceed to further evaluate the franchise. However, if you happen to have run across the franchise opportunity without giving much thought to whether you were impressed with the product or service offered, you need to do some more thinking.

The next step in evaluating a franchise is to focus on what you are receiving in the opportunity. Since you are basically paying for the learning curve of the franchisor, that learning curve or trademarked product needs to be worth something. For large, well-known franchises, the trademarked product or service is very valuable (and expensive too). Other values offered by the franchisor include any below-market supply contracts that the franchisee might have access to.

Whenever you evaluate a franchise opportunity, the same skills and effort that go into business planning (as has been discussed above) should also go into a due diligence effort in evaluating the franchise opportunity. The essential decision that you are focusing on is whether the advantages of using that particular franchise outweigh the cost of franchise fees royalties and other management payments. Just as you use your team of advisers to help with your business, you also want your attorney and accountant to help you review the contract.

Consideration of the franchise begins with the franchise document. Different jurisdictions require different disclosures. In the US, franchisors have to complete a Uniform Franchise Offering Circular which provides all information that would be considered important in making an investment decision. If you live in a jurisdiction that doesn't require franchisors to prepare an offering circular or the franchisor doesn't supply you with a circular, I would not purchase the franchise. There is still much deceit and unfair dealing in areas where franchisors are regulated. I can only imagine the fraud that would occur if there were no regulation or the franchisor did not bother to comply with the existing regulation.

The following are some items of interest in the franchise document:

Right granted

The right that is granted to you is one of the most important parts of the franchise. Often the right to offer the product or service is a territorial right. From your standpoint, the territorial right needs to be broad enough and exclusive enough in defining the market for you to offer the product or service. Lately, there have been some lawsuits with regard to a well-known franchisor who was granting franchise rights too close to existing locations. This had the effect of the various franchise outlets cannibalizing each other. The grant of territorial rights must define a sufficient market to generate a profitable return. Remember our marketing analysis from the earlier chapters. In examining the franchise opportunity, you want to determine whether there is sufficient market within the franchise grant. You also need your attorney to analyse the exclusivity of the rights.

Assistance to the franchisee

The amount of assistance that the franchisor is required to give to the franchisee is important also. Some of the agreements require that the franchisor help with site location. The location is very important, especially with regard to any retail locations. Other assistance would include the training offered to the franchisee. Ideally, the franchise agreement should be fairly specific about the type of training offered. For example, the training should be defined specifically to include both in the classroom and on the job monitoring experience. Training is important because you want the ability to deliver the product to the consumer consistently. Also included in the training could be pre-opening assistance.

Marketing budget

This can be both a grey and sensitive area in the franchise opportunity. Often the contract will specify certain sums of money to be paid by the franchisee for marketing budgets. However, this fund is always controlled by the franchisor who produces material such as newspaper ads, direct-mail pieces and point-of-sale materials and also buys time or space in the various media outlets. Sometimes it is very difficult to be able to translate these amounts expended into direct benefits to the franchisee. Be wary of excessive fees or commissions to the franchisor for the marketing payments.

Purchase of material

Another major benefit of being a franchisee involves the opportunity to buy inventory and goods below market prices. The franchisor has the right to demand certain product specifications with respect to the materials used in the franchise. However, be wary of contracts that insist you buy all of your products from the franchisor.

Operating procedures manual

In many cases, the operating procedures manual is an important asset which also documents the business format. It is basically the 'how to' manual on the business. This is always referred to in the licence agreement and can be grounds for breach by the franchisee.

Term of the agreement

Usually, the franchise is a long-term relationship with a 15 to 20 year agreement. An important clause is renewal rights which would allow the franchisee to continue, assuming that all the conditions of the franchise contract were met. The failure to have a renewal clause in the term of agreement is one of concern since it may indicate that the franchisor is not likely to grant renewals.

Sale of the business

Another important clause in the franchise agreement is any restrictions concerning the sale of the business. As we've discussed in this book, a good harvesting strategy is the sale of the business. However, note that the franchise agreement might restrict the sale of the business and perhaps put a damper on your harvesting plans. Some licences require a right of first refusal by the franchisor or impose a pre-existing buy-out formula.

Legal proceedings

Check to see if there are any pending legal proceedings against the franchisor. This would give you any information about any unfair dealings by the franchisor.

Financial results

Franchisors are generally very reluctant to discuss profit information with you. The reason is that they do not want to be sued if the profit projections are not accurate. However, you can use the break-even analysis from Chapter 11 to try to determine profits. Usually, they will readily supply you with information about unit prices and about fixed and variable costs. With this information, you can calculate break-even volume and unit volume required to reach various levels of profits. Then you can estimate how realistic it will be to reach these unit volume targets. Although they will not give you profit information, you can easily compute the necessary profit information from the available facts on costs and selling price. Break-even in terms of units is determined by the following formula:

$$\frac{\text{Fixed costs}}{\text{selling price per unit } - \text{ variable cost per unit}}$$

Also be aware that in the franchise system, there are always sources of conflict. To begin with, the franchisor normally incurs a lot of costs in setting up the franchise operations. One way to recoup the costs is by selling franchise units. Second, while the franchisor is paid a royalty based upon gross sales, the franchisee takes their profit out of the bottom-line. Although the franchisors have been able to control the market with franchisees, this control is now shifting. Franchisees are generally now better educated and prepared than in the past and are not as hesitant to challenge the franchisor.

Some general checklist points for choosing a franchisor are as follows:

1   Select the proper franchisor, one with either a well-accepted trademark or one with a well-accepted operating system. Make sure that you have a genuine interest in the company.

2   Thoroughly investigate the franchisor. Talk to franchisees, particularly those who have recently left the system. In some areas, the franchisor is required by law to provide such names. Try to meet as many franchise owners in person as you can. Find a good, quiet time to interview them and then ask them all the hard questions about the franchise operation. Also ask the franchisor about any litigation against the company and investigate further. Sometimes a mixed report on the franchisor is actually better than a perfect report. If everyone is giving them glowing reports, then something might not be right.

3   Analyse the franchisor's business and marketing plans. Be sure that advertising and marketing dollars will be spent in your franchise market.

4   Maintain proper records in the event that litigation or disagreements result. Keep a good record of all conversations, including the date, the persons spoken to, and promises made.

5   Have an attorney review the franchise documents. A very important issue to be contractually established is the distance from your franchise that another franchisor can place a competing unit. Another is whether the franchisees are subject to mandatory arbitration.

6   Put everything in writing. Any promise not in writing is just a promise, with no legal effect. Assume that anything that is not put in writing is not binding and don't factor that into your consideration.

7   Have your accountant analyse all the financial data. Do the projections justify the purchase and permit sufficient capital for the startup to pay for the business? Have your accountant determine break-even, both in terms of units and dollars.

8   Compare what you gathered on investigating the franchise with your own analysis as to whether or not the concept will be successful in the marketplace. Who will your competition be? Try to assess how the business will be perceived in your market. Check the demographic information to determine whether there is a growing or declining market in your area. Try to determine how valuable the product or service is.

Some items in your investigation, which should cause you concern are:

■   The franchisor is not adequately protecting the intellectual property. In many cases, a trademark can be very valuable to the franchisees. The franchisor's failure to protect intellectual property is a *big* concern.

■   The franchisor turns out to be thinly capitalized. This is usually reflected on the financial statement and the financial strength of the owner. Do some ratio analysis like a quick and current ratio.

■   There is much litigation against the franchise.

■   The fees of the franchise operation are too high to make any money.

Buying a business

Another way to get into business quickly is to simply buy a business. This allows you to bypass much of the initial work yourself by stepping into the shoes of a going concern which already has in place its customers, suppliers, employees, physical facility in addition to the business. Generally, the ongoing cash flow of the businesses (provided that it is accurate) contains a very clear picture about how the businesses is already doing and what to expect in the future.

Generally, the same due diligence that applies to reviewing a franchisee operation also applies to buying a business. Unfortunately, I have had to counsel more than one person who bought a business only to later find a lot of problems. These problems included the poor condition of the assets, declining merchandise and even undisclosed liabilities. In addition, there were many verbal promises from the seller which were not met. If only the buyer had consulted me *before* they bought their business, I could have protected them better.

The moral of the story is to have a strongly worded purchase agreement that protects you from undisclosed liabilities and provides warranties with respect to all material aspects of the business. Some investigation and due diligence goes a long way also. In addition, you definitely need to consult professional advisers when you're considering buying a business.

Some questions to ask yourself before buying a business:

1   *Am I suited for this business?* Just because a business falls into your lap does not mean you have to run out and buy that business. While the opportunity might be good, be sure that it is a business you are very interested in. You may be doing it for a long time.

2   *What is the real reason the businesses is for sale?* Ideally, the best business to buy would be from the business owner who is making their harvest from the sale and retiring. Perhaps the retiring owner may be able to assist you in the transition and act as a consultant. In other cases, *question* the motives of those selling the business. They'll usually claim that the business is great but that they're ready to move on. But is that the real reason they are selling? Are there undisclosed liabilities? Are their other problems with the business? You need to find that out because otherwise they're going to be *your* problems.

3   What is the replacement cost of the business? Although we discuss valuing the business later, a place to start in valuing the business is its replacement cost.

4   What type of cash flow does the business generate? This is where you have to carefully examine the books and records as well as the tax returns of the owner to see if they are giving you accurate financial information. Never fall victim to the owner who claims to have a secret set of books that reflect the 'true' value of the business. Naturally, that would indicate dishonesty. In addition, any business owner with the audacity to cheat the big government with all of its resources, will certainly cheat you.

5   What else goes along with the business? In evaluating this, you need to determine both assets and liabilities. In particular, be wary of any undisclosed liabilities. That is where your attorney comes into play and make sure that strong representations and warranties are provided by the seller. Your attorney might recommend a purchase of the assets of the business rather then purchasing the business as a going concern. This could have the effect of relieving you of any undisclosed liabilities.

You will also want to determine any assets that would be included with a business. This would include both tangible and intangible assets, including any machinery or equipment, physical structure and any items of inventory that would be included in the business. All of the assets that go with the business should be specified in writing with a proper accounting made of these assets. Be aware of such intangible assets like customer lists, favourable lease arrangements, favourable contractual arrangements. Sometimes these intangible assets can add considerable value to the purchaser PROVIDED that you as a purchaser will be able to take advantage of them. Sometimes contracts and leases do not apply to a purchaser. That is why due diligence must be done to determine which intangible assets and contractual rights flow to the purchaser of the business.

A related intangible that is often overlooked is the impact of replacing the former owner. Is the business going to be able to retain its existing customers? What about the loyalty of the staff? Although your attorney will undoubtedly request a noncompete agreement from the seller, what will be the impact of the seller's departure? Will the seller offer to ease the transition?

6   What are all the important factors behind the business? Before buying the business be sure that you have researched it in the same manner that you would before you start a similar business. Do you understand the industry? The competition? How your business fits in? The keys to making your business successful? Be sure that you understand the important components of the business and what makes the business survive.

Locating the business

Locating a business for sale is not always an easy task. Unlike the sellers of houses, most businesses don't advertise openly for fear of discouraging existing customers. After all, who wants to do business with someone who is 'on the block'? Consequently, the process of purchasing a business is much more subtle and takes more time and effort. Some ways to go about locating a business are as follows:

- *Commercial business brokers.* A commercial business broker can often be one of the best ways of finding a business. Since many ongoing businesses are reluctant to advertise themselves, many businesses are sold through business brokers. A good business broker might have numerous contacts with people in the area who might be considering a sale. Often the broker's commission on the sale will be paid by the seller. In addition, sellers who list their businesses with a broker are generally more realistic on their selling price.

- *Classified advertisements.* Another way to locate a business for sale is in the 'business opportunities' section of newspapers and magazines. Many of the ads there are placed by business brokers. If you're interested in buying a business, skimming through the classifieds can keep you up to date with the market. Some of the ads are placed by buyers also.

- *Professionals.* Your professional network can be of assistance in this area also. Professional advisers such as bankers, accountants and attorneys might have clients selling businesses or the knowledge of businesses for sale. In fact, a banker might be aware of a troubled business that is for sale.

- *Cold calling.* If you happen to come across a business that interests you, it never hurts to ask.

Once you start getting serious about the business, then it is time to bring in your professionals. If the business passes muster on your initial interest, then you might want to commence full-scale negotiations. Be careful about signing anything that would obligate you though. Often a confidentiality agreement is required to see the books and records, which should not present a problem. Sometimes even a deposit is required in the early stages of negotiation.

Valuing the business

Setting a value on a business can sometimes be a little tricky. In many cases, the owner has sacrificed much for the business, which is the owner's 'baby.' Reducing the value of their 'baby' based upon objective standards like cash flow and return on investment can sometimes be a shock to the owner. Sometimes an outside appraiser can set the value. Also, you could make the owner aware that you want to perpetuate the business in the owner's image. This might affect the owner's willingness to compromise and to help you in the formative stages of the business.

There are many approaches to valuing a business. Much of it depends upon the industry. Usually the true value of the business converges somewhere between the three techniques. The techniques are based on the types of financial statements that we saw earlier in the book. One method used to value the business is its book value, which is based on the balance sheet of the business. Another way to value the business is also based on assets, but uses replacement cost instead of book value. The final way to value a business is based upon its net annual cash flow from the cash flow statement.

Book value

The book value is very similar to the owner's equity in that liabilities are subtracted from assets to determine net book value. However, some of the problems with using book value is that the assets are valued at historical cost. The use of the book value does not reflect any appreciation in the assets or the ability of the assets to generate income. In addition, book value can sometimes overlook the value of intangible assets, which often comprise the healthy part of the value of the business.

Replacement cost

This method values the business through the replacement cost of the assets. Replacement cost does remedy a deficiency in the book value method in that it does take into account asset appreciation. The replacement cost is a good measure of how much it would cost in today's market to replace the business. However, the replacement cost does not value the intangible assets or take into account the ability of the business to generate cash.

Cash flow

Unlike the two previous balance sheet measures, the cash-flow method focuses on the cash flow of the business. As opposed to valuing the assets of the business, you are focusing upon the return that is given to the owner. The business is valued by taking its net cash flow for a specific number of years. This specific number is referred to as the multiple. The formula for value is cash flow × multiple. The multiple is dependent on the type of industry, the condition of the industry, its competition, and profit level. Multiples normally range from four to six, although they can have a much wider range. Usually, experienced business brokers will have an idea of the multiples for the particular industry.

Another item which affects the price of the business is the negotiating position. Naturally the owner who wants to quickly sell the business might take less for a cash offer.

Summary

1   Franchising and buying a business are alternative methods of entry into the world of business ownership.

2   Although both franchising and buying a business are shortcuts, don't shortcut your evaluation process of them. Determine that the businesses are suitable for you and exercise due diligence in your review of the opportunities.

3   Evaluate the franchise and ongoing business just as you would your own startup.

4   Obtain competent professional assistance in evaluating any business opportunity.

CHAPTER SEVENTEEN

Self management fundamentals – strategies for personal excellence

> Never give up. Never never give up.
>
> (Winston Churchill)

So far we have examined many business management principles. However, all the business management principles in the world will not guarrantee success for the business owner who suffers from poor 'self management' techniques. The owner has to practise effective self management in addition to proper business management. The pressures on today's business owner are overwhelming. In addition to under-standing the intricacies of their business, the business owner has to wear a variety of hats, even with the help of good advisers. In the beginning, the business is essentially the alter ego of the owner. The performance of the business greatly depends on the owner's performance. Consequently, the failure of the owner to manage themselves, could adversely affect the business.

There is a wealth of information on what I refer to as self management. Other terms used include peak performance, leadership and motivation. I first became acquainted with the peak performance concepts in 1985 through audiotapes. One author who I really liked was Brian Tracy. He had an effective, hard-hitting style and his presentations were saturated with outstanding information on personal effectiveness. His material has had a profound impact on my life, and Mr Tracy has been good enough to let me share some of it with you later in this chapter. In addition, I listened to other authors and quickly became a motivational tape junkie. Soon my bookcases, closets and automobile were filled with educational and inspirational material. What I have learned during my 13 years with the experts was that certain self-management strategies could definitely assist in managing your performance and achieving business success. I have divided the self-management strategies into what I like to call the 'seven bases of success'. These seven bases include:

1   knowledge base;

2   direction base;

3   emotional base;

4   spiritual base;

5   financial base;

6   physical base;

7   relationship base.

Seven bases of success

Knowledge base

Since we are currently in an information age, the value of knowledge cannot be overestimated. The fact that you are reading this book shows that you are serious about obtaining knowledge about business startups. It was the goal of this book to impart a fairly comprehensive amount of business management knowledge and practices to enable you to successfully plan your business. However, do be aware that your knowledge base with respect to business planning does not end here. There is not a single book that contains everything that one needs to know about managing their business. Every one of us has to constantly update our skills and knowledge.

For example, you have to keep up to date with your industry trends as well as those in your market. As a business owner, it is also helpful to keep up with the general state of business. Make it a practice to at least go through the leading business periodicals in your area. I subscribe to *Business Week, The Economist, Inc. Magazine, Entrepreneur, The Wall Street Journal* as well some local and speciality publications. Subscribe to the business publications in your area. Also keep current with those publications that target your industry.

Resolve to commit to a process of lifelong learning. In order to keep my knowledge base current, I read over a dozen periodicals as well as between 75 and 100 books annually. Now don't gasp, since this is not as impossible as it sounds. I skim through most of the periodicals. I first check the table of contents to determine which articles are of particular interest. I take the time to read those articles, but generally skim the rest. If an article is important enough, I'll tear it out or photocopy it and then scan it into my computer. Scanning is an optical recognition process, whereby articles and other images can be scanned into a computer and saved. I'll talk more about scanning in the next chapter. With regards to the books, my secret weapon is audio cassette tapes. Most of the books I get through, I actually listen to on tape. In addition, I can listen to tapes while I am doing something else, like driving an automobile. One service that I subscribe to sends me, on a monthly basis, condensed versions of two leading business books on audio tape. That is about one-third of my book goal right there. The other tapes I either order or rent from the library or rental outlets.

Listening to audio tapes is an outstanding way to leverage time, since you can listen to them while you are driving, exercising, on an aeroplane and even while relaxing. The key is to use your down time productively. You'd be surprised how this time accumulates and how much you can learn during these intervals. I know I was. Take advantage of those hours behind the wheel or other periods of down time. Listen to inspirational and educational audio tapes.

Another part of keeping your knowledge base current is keeping up with technology. I will discuss in more detail the benefits of becoming 'powered up' in the next chapter. As we saw in Chapter 5, the on-line world is opening up a vast knowledge domain, which you cannot afford to ignore. So acquaint yourself with the new knowledge frontiers of the Internet. This can be a tremendous source of important knowledge and information. But as I recommended in Chapter 5, don't ignore the traditional sources of knowledge either. Make it a practice to periodically visit your local library.

Direction base

The next base of success is your direction base, which involves establishing the direction for your business and your life and then following through on your plans. Of course, much of the focus of this book was to provide your business with a sense of direction in the form of a business plan. A good business plan establishes your direction by plotting the course of your business. The next step is to follow through and actually do the activities set out in the plan. A business plan will be of no help if it is not implemented. A strategy for implementing your business plan is as follows:

1   Go through your business plan and note all of the activities or plans either listed in the 'action steps' or in the plan itself that have not been done. For example, part of your marketing plan might include designing a web site or preparing a brochure. Or your management portion might indicate that you will establish a banking relationship within a certain period of time. If you have not already done so, break these plans into activities. For example, preparing a brochure might involve the use of a marketing consultant, printer, logo design and preparation of brochure copy. Break out all of the separate activities.

2   Once you have made a list of all the activities, schedule a time to do them and then proceed to do them.

3   As you develop other ideas and strategies for your business, go though the same process. Break out the ideas into the activities necessary to implement them. Schedule the activities and do them.

4   Use your business plan or perhaps an appendix to keep track of any new strategies and the activities necessary to implement them. You don't have to necessarily rewrite your plan with any changes or new strategies. Perhaps keep track of your changes in an appendix. Your main goal is to use your plan as a working document in a way that makes sense to you.

5   Repeat the process. Develop plans. Break the plans up into activities. Schedule the activities. Do the activities.

Although this system of setting and following through on your business plan goals and activities can be tedious, it is not particularly complicated. Your main challenge is to establish a system to keep track of your plans, strategies, and activities. As suggested, you might want to use an appendix to your business plan. In addition, as we will discuss in the next chapter, there are a lot of personal information manager systems for computers which can help you keep track of your list of activities. But no matter what system you choose, choose a system that makes sense to you. If you are used to preparing to-do lists on loose leaf paper, then by all means continue this process. I once experimented with an elaborate life-planning system which used various colour-code charts and schedules to break down and implement life goals. Although my intentions were good, the system proved a little too cumbersome for me and I ended up not keeping up with it. So in following through on your business plan, use a system that works the best for you.

Systems like the one outlined above can be also thought of as time management systems. The system makes the best use of your time by focusing on the important activities. Every business owner has considerable time pressure and it can be very difficult to get to everything. There are tasks left undone in even the most productive of lives. Consequently, it is important that you establish and use a system of planning important activities and then following though. Without such a system, the important activities of the business could often get lost in the crush of the day. The system helps you prioritize the important projects.

An important corollary to effective time management is to not delay on important items. Learn to do the important things NOW! If something strikes you as important – do it now. If you find out that a large prospect is in the market for your type of product or service, contact them immediately. Don't put it off until you're 'ready.' Even if you are a little intimidated, contact them anyway. In my own case, when I was writing this chapter, I realized that many of the ideas espoused by Brian Tracy would be very useful. However, if I was going to quote his ideas, I was going to need his permission. Although I considered him somewhat as my personal guru and had practically memorized his presentations, I didn't know him. Naturally, I was a little intimidated at the thought of contacting him about using his material. It certainly was something that I could have easily put off. But I decided to go ahead and contact him immediately. I remembered that, like myself, Tracy was a member of the National Speakers Association. I located his fax number in the NSA directory and then faxed him a short letter identifying myself and requesting his permission to use some of his materials. Within a couple of days, he faxed back his permission. I wonder if I would have ended up following through on the thought if I had delayed. The moral of the story is that if you get an important idea – act on it immediately!

Another time-management suggestion is to keep an organized workspace. How much time have you wasted trying to find things in a disorganized office? Stay vigilant in keeping your work space neat. I find that my scanner has helped me remove much of the clutter from my desk. All those message slips, business cards, articles and scraps of paper that used to litter my desk, now get sucked up right into the scanner. Another big help in reducing the need for paper are computer networks and e-mail. Use them whenever your budget will allow. I will discuss networks and e-mail further in the next chapter.

Emotional base

The next base of success is your emotional base. The business owner needs to remain emotionally grounded to withstand the 'slings and arrows of outrageous fortune' that often accompany self employment. It is those entrepreneurs who remain cool under pressure, who not only survive, but who generally thrive in a competitive environment. Others who become easily frazzled, tend to make unnecessary mistakes.

Consequently, managing your emotional state is important for the business owner. One critical aspect of your emotional base that cannot be overstated is your *attitude*. Just about every self-help source that I know strongly emphasizes the importance of attitude. Simply put, your attitude determines your emotional state. Those people with a positive and optimistic attitude tend to respond better to adversity. On the other hand, those who are negative and pessimistic don't respond as well. So resolve to remain positive and optimistic, even in the face of the inevitable setbacks. As Abraham Lincoln said, people are generally as happy as they set out to be.

Some tips in maintaining a proper attitude is to make it a habit of turning challenges into opportunities. Resolve to bounce back from short-term defeats. Don't dwell on your failures. Learn from them, but keep the tuition low. In addition, use a positive coping stategy to deal with stressful situations. Coping behaviours can be divided into two types, control oriented and escape oriented. Control-oriented coping is considered more positive since it focuses on solving the particular problem. Escape-oriented coping focuses more on the particular emotional distress. During difficult times, focus your attention on finding solutions rather than worrying about the situations.

Spiritual base

At the risk of making an abrupt 'new age' turn in this book, I am going to recommend the benefits of having a spiritual base. During the hectic world of the entrepreneur, it helps greatly to step back and gain some perspective on the world as a whole with a regular spiritual practice. This regular spiritual practice can be in the form of prayer, meditation or some other type of contemplation exercise. The practice can be anything which allows you to pause and reflect. Slowing down to reflect and seek spiritual renewal can often be difficult for the busy entrepreneur. But it is well worth the effort. Not only can a regular spiritual practice quiet the mind and produce inner peace, but it can also produce inner strength to draw from during times of adversity.

I learned to appreciate the importance of a regular spiritual practice not that long ago. Although I had regularly attended church services, I never really tapped fully into spirituality as a way to replenish the soul and provide comfort. During a difficult period, I finally realized just how important my faith really was. Not only did my religious beliefs help to sustain me, but the spiritual practice also provided important insights and guidance. I now pay much more attention to my faith and even attend a silent retreat once a year at the Manresa House of Retreats in Convent, Louisiana. Not only do I receive much spiritual nourishment, but as a bonus I even get a few good business ideas.

Your method of spiritual practice is completely a matter of personal preference. Ideally, the practice should quiet your mind and provide you with a certain amount of perspective and inner peace. Anything which refreshes the soul can assist you in facing the rigours of the day. Take the time to refresh and renew yourself. If you have never meditated before, there are certain instructional guides. However, the spiritual practice does not have to be complicated. It can be as simple as a regular walk in the park or 10 minutes in silence each morning. The point is to quiet your mind and then listen.

Physical base

Entrepreneurs need considerable physical stamina. The hours as a business owner are generally taxing and long. There is also a lot of stress involved. Consequently, you need to be in top physical condition. The three ingredients for a good physical base are a proper diet, physical exercise and rest.

Fad diets come and go and end up confusing people with conflicting information about calories and fat grams. However a good diet is mostly common sense. Try to balance your diet and avoid too much refined sugar or fats. Fresh fruits and vegetables are important staples. It is better to eat several smaller meals than to gorge yourself at one. Limit your consumption of caffeine, nicotine and alcohol.

A basic exercise regimen can provide enormous health benefits and reduce stress. This regimen could include some cardiovascular and resistance exercises for at least 30 minutes for three times a week.

The final component of a good physical regimen is adequate rest. Determine the amount of sleep that you need and resolve to get it. Remember that you can only go so long without proper rest.

Financial base

The next base of success is your financial base. While much of your efforts and energy is going to be directed at your business, don't neglect to establish a personal savings plan outside your business. You may not be able to contribute much, if anything, at first. Still, focus on building up your personal savings to the extent that you can. Sometimes getting your money out of your business is not always a guaranteed prospect. You might not be able to readily sell your business. That is why you need to have a personal savings plan also. As you begin to draw an adequate salary from your business, commit a portion to your personal savings. Set up a deferred tax free savings plan, if they are permitted in your area.

People are generally living longer and are going to need more assets to sustain them during retirement. The sooner you plan for this, the better off you will be.

Relationship base

I said earlier that no entrepreneur is an island. Although we were talking then about business advisers, entrepreneurs also need personal relationships to sustain them. The first priority in relationships includes their spouse and family. Next there are friends and associates. Starting a business can often take its toll on relationships. While much of your energy should and will be directed at your business, don't turn your back on the important people in your life. Understand that your business affects the entire family and that they too are paying a price. Remember that all the business success in the world will not give you any satisfaction without the loved ones to enjoy it with. Although you will be busy, particularly in the beginning, do set aside some *quality* time to be with the people that matter in your life. During this time focus on them and not your business.

Summary

1   Proper self management is just as important to your business as proper business management.

2   A good self management strategy can be built on the seven bases of success, which are

(a) knowledge base;

(b) direction base;

(c) emotional base

(d) spiritual base;

(e) financial base;

(f) physical base;

(g) relationship base.

The following material is a synopsis of a programme entitled 'Psychology of Success' by Brian Tracy. I think that this programme is one of the best self-development audiotapes on the market. I've summarized this below. I express my sincere thanks to Brian Tracy for letting me reproduce his programme here.

PSYCHOLOGY OF SUCCESS

By Brian Tracy

(Reprinted with Permission of Brian Tracy, Brian Tracy International, 462 Stevens Ave., #202, Solana Beach, California, 92075, phone (619) 481-2977/fax (619) 481-2445)

I Introduction

1   Success begins inside you. It is a state of mind. It is a function of your character and personality.

2   The psychology of success equals mental fitness; it is a feeling of self-confidence, happiness, enthusiasm and a positive mental attitude.

3   Your level of self esteem is the foundation quality for all success, all high achievement, and all peak performance.

4   The purposeful development of self esteem is the psychology of success.

5   True self esteem arises from an enhanced feeling of competence.

6   Self esteem is largely determined by how much you believe in yourself. Beliefs determine your reality and beliefs edit out all information inconsistent with them. It is important to change one's belief to believe that you are capable of great success.

7   One's level of self esteem is determined by how much one believes oneself to be confident, worthwhile, respected and important. Every experience which causes you to feel more valuable and worthwhile raises your self esteem and every experience which causes you to feel less valuable lowers your self esteem.

8   The opposite of self esteem is fear, stress, psychosomatic illness, personality problems, negativity, defeat and failure in life.

9   It is possible to change your beliefs and feelings about yourself by feeding your mind with a steady stream of positive constructive messages that are consistent with the outcomes that you desire, rather than the outcomes that you fear. You do become what you think about most.

10   It is important that you use positive self talk; that you repeat with enthusiasm and conviction. One must emotionalize the things that you say to yourself e.g. 'I believe something wonderful is going to happen to me today'.

11   Practise visualization of yourself with the qualities, attributes and behaviour that you desire. Before going to sleep every night visualize accomplishment, enjoyment, etc.

12   Affirmation + visualization + positive expectation =

(a) A positive optimistic and cheerful person
(b) The attraction of people and circumstances into your life in harmony with your dominant thoughts (the law of attraction)

13   Feed your mind continually with positive books, magazines, tapes, videos and seminars. Avoid negative books, magazines, tapes and people.

14   Associate with positive, cheerful and success-oriented people.

15   It is important to act the part; pattern your conduct and behaviour after successful people. Even if you don't feel like a success; act like a success. If you act self confident you will feel self confident.

16   Summary:

(a) Success is not an accident – it is predictable; it can be learned and it can be learned by anyone.
(b) If you want to be a success, you should use proven successful methods for becoming successful.
(c) The majority of people fail in life.

(d) Your level of self esteem is the most important determinant of success.

(e) Everyone suffers self doubt, guilt and fear of failure or rejection – it is successful people who master these fears.

(f) You do become what you think about most.

(g) If you act like you are successful, fake it until you make it, pretend: you will begin to think like a successful person.

II Psychology of failure

1   It is basic human nature to be lazy, ambitious, selfish, greedy and vain and to do things in an expedient fashion. In order to be successful you must resist the expediency factor (E-factor).

2   Successful people make the habit of doing the things that unsuccessful people do not do.

3   Every act resisting expediency reinforces the habit of self discipline and leads to success.

4   The ability to delay gratification in the short term and concentrate on long-term goals determines one's success.

III The principle of purpose

1   The way to rid yourself of the E-Factor is to focus on achievable goals, which must be clear and defined and which are challenging and which you have many reasons to achieve. It is important to make goal setting a habit.

2   The best way to overcome fear and stress is by reaching and achieving short-term and intermediate goals.

IV Principle of excellence

1   You are never truly fulfilled in life until you make the commitment to become excellent at what you do and specialize in one particular area.

2   Being excellent is to become marginally better in many aspects of the activity as opposed to much better in one particular aspect.

3   After every performance, ask yourself two things:

(a) What did I do correctly?

(b) How can I do it better?

4   Never focus upon what you did wrong since it would become fixed in your subconscious.

V Principle of responsibility

1   Winners take full responsibility for all events and actions; losers try to blame others.

2   If something goes wrong, winners look for solutions and losers look for who to blame.

3   Treat your job as if you are self employed; everyone is president of their own personal services corporation.

VI Principle of service

1   You presently live in a service economy. Since we are not Robinson Crusoe, we depend upon others to survive and all that we have to offer in exchange for goods and services that we need are our personal services.

2   Ralph Waldo Emerson stated that everything that we give out in the universe comes back to us; what we sow we will reap.

3   Remember that one works forty hours a week for survival and works the rest of the week for success. Hard work is the real key to success.

4   One is never truly fulfilled until one is immersed in the task of doing worthwhile things in serving others.

VII Principle of concentration

1   The principle of concentration can be summarized in making a habit of: (a) setting out a list of priority activities and (b) focusing on each separate priority, giving it your full undivided attention and resolving to not stop working on it until it is finished.

2   Resist giving attention to the urgent as opposed to the important.

VIII Principle of cooperation

1   You must make the habit of really listening to other people.

IX Principle of creativity

1   Everyone is born a genius, which is not dependent upon IQ, but on the ability to use one's mental faculties. People are using only a small percentage of their mental faculties.

2   The three qualities of genius are as follows: (i) an open, almost childlike mind which is able to consider many possibilities for attacking the situation; (ii) the ability to concentrate and focus on a single problem or situation (iii) a systematic, orderly and analytical way of approaching all problems.

3   Creativity favours a relaxed mind. Look for the good in each situation and find something positive in every adversity or setback. Creativity is stimulated by (i) intense and desired goals, (ii) pressing problems, and (iii) focused questions.

4   Approaches to problem solving.

(a) Write out your most pressing problem on a clean sheet of paper preferably in the morning. Formulate the problem into a question and write 20 answers to the question. Sometimes the last one is worth more than the other 19 combined. Select one and implement it immediately.

(b) Write out a clear answer to the question, what am I trying to avoid in a certain situation?

(c) Systematic steps to problem solving:

- approach a problem as though there is a single positive solution to it;
- use positive language. Refer to the problem as a situation or opportunity or challenge;
- define the problem clearly;
- define the causes for the particular situation;
- identify all possible solutions to the problem, including the obvious and the not so obvious;
- once you have made a decision, take action;
- assign specific responsibility to solve the problem,
- set deadlines for completion; take action immediately
- approach to solving problems:
  - write down what you are trying to do, accomplish, avoid, etc.;
  - write down how you are trying to do this;
  - write down your basic assumptions;
  - are these assumptions wrong? Suppose one did the opposite – zero base thinking;
- Summary: there are many opportunities to innovate. All you have to be is ten per cent new in any time of innovation to be successful. Creativity begins with you and creativity favours a prepared and relaxed mind; do things a

little better; trust your intuition which favours your true intention; and learn from your mistakes.

X Principle of self development

1   Resolve to make yourself a perpetual learning machine; read, study, attend seminars and listen to audio cassette tapes.

2   Remain open to new ideas; remain curious and interested.

3   Associate with successful people, learn from them.

4   Study success, repeat proven methods that have worked for others.

5   You need to always grow with the input of new ideas, otherwise you will stagnate.

6   Work as hard on yourself as you do on your job.

7   Personal development is a springboard to proven excellence and high achievement. In addition, the self respect and self confidence from self development put one on the road to success.

XI Principle of integrity

1   Every addition to the truth subtracts from it.

2   Whatever you give away will multiple ten fold and come back to you.

3   Always do what is right and moral in the eyes of man.

XII Principle of courage

1   Your principal goal in life is to develop your full potential and become everything you can be. Everyone suffers from fear of failure, fear of loss, etc. If fear becomes a dominant emotion in your life you will never achieve success. Therefore, courage is indispensable in that it controls fear and overcomes fear with desire.

   (a) Principles to develop courage

      – The fear of failure is a learned habit. The way to conquer it is to face the thing that you fear the most; death of fear will then result.
      – Most fear is caused by ignorance; the more you learn, the less fear you will have. It is important to get the facts.

- When confronted with a fearful situation, step back and get organized. This will help you deal with the fear.
- Always think of the worst thing that could happen in any situation and develop alternatives in the event of that contingency.
- Act decisively. Make firm commitments. Make decisive actions based on those commitments. 'Act boldly and unseen forces will come to your aid.'
- Neutralize the fear of failure by using visualization and positive affirmation. Reprogramme for success. When confronted with a difficult, fearful situation repeat 'I can do it' repeatedly until the fear subsides.
- Move confidently in the direction of your own dreams. Act as though it is impossible to fail.
- The flip side of courage is persistence which is self discipline in action and the courage to achieve. Your willingness to persist is a true measure of your belief in self and your belief in your ability to succeed. Adversity should be embraced and then overcome since every adversity contains a certain positive element. It is impossible to go through life without confronting some adversity. There is a way that one handles adversity which leads to one's ultimate success.
- Remember Churchill's famous saying 'never give up; never never give up'. You should believe that every set-back is a spur to a greater effort. Believe that you were put on earth to make a difference and use temporary defeat as another way of learning how to succeed. Remember that the psychology of success is to always do what you should do when you should do it whether you like it or not and whether you feel like it or not.

■ CHAPTER EIGHTEEN ■

Technology basics – get powered up NOW!

> The only limit to our realization of tomorrow will be our
> doubts of today.
>
> (Franklin D. Roosevelt)

For those of you who are not yet using computers, let me urge you to get powered up NOW! The cost of computers is just too small and their benefits too large to put them off any longer. Computers can save you both time and money in your business. They can pay for themselves many times over. Below is a discussion of computer hardware, software, peripherals and applications.

Hardware

The hardware prices for computers keep dropping dramatically. You can now buy a fully powered unit for a fraction of the price of just a few months ago. In addition, if your budget is really limited, look for a used computer. While the Pentium chip (and its offspring) is the new industry standard, computers with a 486 chip can handle the majority of small business needs. Although they can be a little slow, they can be fine for the basic user. You could probably pick up a 486 *very* inexpensively.

There are three important components to a computer's hardware. The first is the microprocessor, which can be thought of as the engine that drives the computer. It is expressed in megahertz (Mhz). While the industry standard is now over 200 Mhz, it is possible to get by with less should your computer needs not involve heavy graphics or complicated technical programs. The next item of interest is the size of the hard drive. With new software taking up more and more space, you need to get a hard drive of at least one and maybe two gigabytes. The final important component is random access memory, which is known as RAM. Your RAM will determine how well your computer runs. Usually 16 megabytes will be sufficient, although 32 megabytes will make your machine run much better.

These are some of the main factors in the price of the computer. If your budget is limited, compromise on one of the above. Don't let someone oversell computer features. However, you also want something that will last you for a while. Do your best within your budget and keep your eye open for new computers. I see ads all the time in the newspaper practically *giving* away older models.

Usually, the purchase of a printer accompanies your computer. Like computers, printers have become less expensive and better. If you are not worried about colour, then even a used printer might serve your needs. In addition, the inkjet printers are now printing in high-quality colour as well as black and white. Their price is generally very reasonable. The prices of the higher-quality laser printers have also come down significantly.

Software

Many computers come with a basic software package. Most computers today come with Windows software, which is a graphical computer interface. Some of the types of software that will be of help to you include the following.

Financial/accounting software

One of the main applications for your business would be some type of accounting software that you can use to keep track of the operations of your business. There are numerous accounting packages on the market and you need one that will accommodate your business. Some of the packages can be quite basic, while others are more sophisticated. Before you purchase any type of financial or accounting package, be sure to go through it with your accountant. It would be very helpful to use compatible or even the same financial software as your accountant.

Word processing

Depending upon your type of operations, you'll probably use word-processing software to write letters or other communications and most of all to prepare your business plan. Although Windows comes with a word-processing package, you might want to consider one of the more popular commercial products such as Word or WordPerfect. This would give you wide capabilities in preparing mass mailings and documents, as well as some basic desktop publishing.

Spreadsheet program

The spreadsheet program is similar to your accounting program. However the spreadsheet is limited to the preparation of items in a spreadsheet format and would be ideal to use to prepare pro forma financial statements. But the accounting programs can be used to run a business, prepare income statements and print invoices.

Online services

With the proliferation of the Internet, the use of online services is very popular. The services they provide range from Internet access to hosting your web site. The prices of online services vary and the services offer different benefits. The two major benefits that you are interested in are e-mail and Internet access.

Internet access is becoming increasingly important and useful for the small businesses. There is a common belief among entrepreneurs that the Internet, online research and e-mail are becoming standard business practices. Note that many small businesses have been using the Internet or have become increasingly reliant on its services. In 1996, 2.2 per cent of small businesses had web sites. This number grew to 9 per cent at the end of 1997.

I think that e-mail or electronic mail will continue to grow as a source of communication. It is just too convenient, cheap and reliable. As we saw in Chapter 5, the Internet can also be a good research tool.

Peripherals

Peripherals are the items that can be used with your computer to provide different types of applications.

Scanner

I've already spoken many times about a scanner. The scanner is a separate device that hooks into your computer and allows you to scan images into your computer. As scanners have become less expensive and more accurate, it is now possible to scan documents and have them saved in a word-processing format. Also you can scan in images and pictures to be placed on documents. Scanning is another way to save journal articles and periodical articles. Some entrepreneurs are using scanners to scan graphics and then build their web pages.

Fax modems

Being able to send faxes from your computer can save you a lot of effort. While the fax capability is still very important, it is the modem that is your connection to the online world. It is through the modem that you connect with the various servers or online services to hook you into the Internet. Your modem is also the way that you send e-mail. Once you begin to use e-mail, you will wonder how you ever did without it.

Multi-functional devices

The multi-functional device combines several functions, such as faxing, printing and copying into a small machine primarily designed for small businesses with limited space. Some multi-functional devices also come equipped with a scanner. They have proved popular with small businesses who just need basic functions. Note that the multi-functional device is not suggested for those companies with heavy copying needs.

Additional software

Desktop publishing

Desktop publishing can very helpful to the small business. While the desktop publishing programs are good, they can be very complicated and difficult to use. Sometimes you can do better with a graphical artist.

Contact manager

The contact manager can be a helpful addition to the small business. Anyone who deals with various customers and potential prospects can organize them on a contact manager. In addition, the contact manager can also carry your calendar and schedule your appointments. Another name for contact managers that serve these functions are personal information managers. Some of the sample programs are Goldmine, Act and FileMaker pro.

The contact manager not only lists contacts by their address, phone, fax, e-mail, etc. but also allows you to divide your contacts by certain criteria. In addition, you can cross reference and send mailings to a segment of the mailing list. The contact manager is an excellent way to stay in touch with your client base and to quickly generate mailings and targeted information.

Voice recognition software

One of the more impressive advances in the computer area is voice recognition software. I did part of this book with voice recognition software and even dictated this very sentence. Although the earlier voice recognition packages were both expensive and slow, like so many things in the computer industry, its prices have dropped while its quality has increased. It will not be too long before voice recognition software is commonplace in many computer applications. However, now it is certainly affordable for the small business. If part of your job involves a great deal of writing, then voice recognition software is well worth the effort. The only catch is that your computer needs to be on the high-end, multimedia scale and contain such extras as a sound card. In addition, it has to be at least a Pentium 133 with 32 megabytes of RAM.

Summary

1   Computers are a necessity for the small business. If you cannot afford a new computer, buy a used one. In any case, find one.

2   The main parts of a computer are the microprocessor, the hard drive capacity and the RAM.

3   The main uses of the computer for the small business include accounting, word processing, spreadsheet and online services.

CHAPTER NINETEEN

Looking beyond your business: estate planning and your exit strategy

> The entrepreneur is essentially a visualizer and an actualizer
> . . . He can visualize something, and when he visualizes it he
> sees exactly how to make it happen.
>
> (Robert L. Schwartz)

All good things must come to an end and the same applies to your business. Obviously, you will not be able to run your business forever. Therefore, it is always wise to keep an exit strategy in the back of your mind. Remember to begin with the end in mind. Although it may seem premature to start talking about your exit strategy, just when you're getting your business off the ground, it is never too early to plan. It is best to develop strategies to maximize the value of your business in the beginning. In addition, if you think you will pass the business down through generations, then you can take some steps now to ensure that your estate plan is in place.

Entrepreneurial education

As we saw in Chapter 18, knowledge is important to the entrepreneur. As business owners you should commit to lifelong learning, particularly in your industry. Now leading business schools are actually presenting courses on entrepreneurship, something which they ignored not that long ago. In addition, there always various courses and seminars on small business. Attend them and see what you can learn. Often the government will sponsor small business workshops. I've spoken several times in this book about Premier FastTrac®, which is an outstanding programme for small businesses. The programme is presently offered throughout the United States and is expanding into foreign countries. The Premier FastTrac® materials were authored by Courtney Price, PhD., R. Mack Davis and the late Dr Richard H. Buskirk. The programme is sponsored by the Kauffman Center for Entrepreneurial Leadership at the Ewing Marion Kauffman Foundation. The late Mr Kauffman was an extremely successful entrepreneur himself, who generously endowed the foundation to promote entrepreneurship. This book is dedicated to his memory.

Exit strategy

One of the advantages of beginning with the end in mind is that you can prepare for it. If you're thinking down line for a harvest strategy, you can take the steps now that will assist you in the process. Although you can plan for a good exit strategy, nothing is guaranteed. That is why I recommended a personal financial strategy to build your personal savings outside the business. However, you do stand a much better chance of obtaining a good harvest if you do plan.

Your first priority in building your business is to build up your market share and cash flow. As we saw in Chapter 16, cash flow is one of the keys to determine a value for the business. Your next priority would be building value in the business itself. What are the steps that you can take to build up value in the business? Some strategies include the purchase of hard assets like real estate and major equipment. Often the business quarters is one of the largest parts of its value. Another way to build value into your business is through the use of business systems. Anytime that you can reduce your business to a process and a system that can be used by others, you have created value. In this case, you are selling knowledge as a process. This is an area that you must go over carefully with your accountant. What type of information or operating system can I integrate into my operations which creates value?

Another critical item in the sale of the business is timing. Depending upon how market and industry conditions change, the value of a business can be affected dramatically. We saw in Chapter 16 how a multiple was used in addition to cash flow to value a business. During good times for your industry, your multiple would generally be high. For example, the multiple right now for radio stations in the US is extremely high. If you own a radio station, now would be the perfect time to sell since the market is valuing radio stations at an all time high. Should you wait, you may never see the same values. That is the value of a harvest strategy, to always think about when it is the best time to harvest.

Estate planning

Estate planning can be thought of as the ultimate exit strategy. Generally, there are a few items that you can address with respect to your business to ensure that your heirs are protected.

If you're in business with someone else, then you need to plan for any untimely death or disability of your partner. Otherwise, you may end up in partnership with your former partner's spouse. The types of ways that you plan for multiple owners is through cross-purchase agreements. Should an owner die or become disabled, the remaining partner would have the option of purchasing their interests. Sometimes, this cross-purchase agreement is funded with insurance proceeds.

Whatever your age, it is important to have a will, particularly if your business is a significant part of the estate. The will basically sets forth how your property is distributed. A major portion of your estate could be your business. Other purposes of a will include the minimizing of estate taxes in those areas that tax estates. Later, as your business grows, you might need to consider some further estate planning strategies to reduce potential estate tax.

Final thoughts

While this book has tried to address all of the areas which I thought were important to the small business, no one book can cover everything. It is my sincere hope that you're better off for having read this book and can approach the business planning process in a more logical and systematic format. I also hope that if you are serious about starting your business, then you will take the time to prepare a business plan. It WILL be worth it! The best of luck to you.

Bibliography

Allen, M. (1995) *Visionary Business: An Entrepreneur's Guide to Success*, New World Library, Novato, CA.

Anthony, R. (1991) *Doing What You Should Love: The Ultimate Key to Personal Happiness and Financial Freedom*, Berkeley Books, New York.

Bolles, R.N. (1997) *What Color is Your Parachute?* Ten Speed Press, Berkeley.

Bygrave, W. (ed) (1992) *The Portable MBA in Entrepreneurship*, John Wiley & Sons, Inc, New York.

Drucker, P. (1995) *Managing In A Time of Great Change,* Dutton, New York.

Harper, S. (1991) *The McGraw-Hill Guide to Starting Your Own Business – a Step-by-Step Blueprint for the First-Time Entrepreneur*, McGraw-Hill, New York.

Falkenstein, L. (1996) *Nichecraft – Using Your Specialness to Focus Your Business, Corner Your Market, and Make Your Customers Seek You Out*, HarperBusiness, New York.

Floyd, E. (1997) *Marketing with Newsletters*, Newsletter Resources, St. Louis.

Horner, J. (1993) *Powermarketing for Small Business*, Oasis Press, Grants Pass, Oregon.

Kiam, V. (1986) *Going For It. How to Succeed As an Entrepreneur,* Morrow, New York.

Levinson, J.C. (1990) *Guerrilla Marketing Weapons: 100 Affordable Marketing Methods for Maximizing Profits From Your Small Business*, Plume, New York.

Livingstone, J.L.(ed) (1992) *The Portable MBA in Finance and Accounting,* John Wiley & Sons, Inc, New York.

Research references

International Encyclopaedia of Associations (1997), Gale Research, Detroit.
Lifestyle and Market Analysis (1996), CACI Marketing Systems, Arlington, VA.
Robert Morris & Associates' Annual Statement Studies (1996), Morris and Associates, Philadelphia, PA.
Small Business Sourcebook (1998), Gale Research, Detroit.
The Sourcebook of Zip Code Demographics (1996), CACI Marketing Systems, Arlington, VA.

Index